Designing Secure
Systems

Designing Secure Systems

Michael Melone

CRC Press
Taylor & Francis Group
Boca Raton London New York

CRC Press is an imprint of the
Taylor & Francis Group, an **informa** business

First edition published 2021
by CRC Press
6000 Broken Sound Parkway NW, Suite 300, Boca Raton, FL 33487–2742

and by CRC Press
2 Park Square, Milton Park, Abingdon, Oxon, OX14 4RN

ISBN: 9780367700010 (hbk)
ISBN: 9780367700027 (pbk)
ISBN: 9781003144182 (ebk)

Typeset in Caslon
by Apex CoVantage, LLC

Any views or opinions represented in this book are personal and belong solely to the author. These views do not represent those of people, institutions, or organizations that the owner may or may not be associated with in a professional or personal capacity.

This book is dedicated to my wife

Jennifer and my daughter Siena

Contents

Acknowledgments

I'd like to thank a number of people who have helped me put this book together over the past few years. First, I'd like to thank my colleagues and friends Kshitij Kumar, Katherine Wu, Christopher Kirk, Cameron Colvin, and John Nix for being my sounding boards for many of the ideas in this book. Your outside perspective really helped shape the content that manifested throughout its development.

I'd also like to thank Chris Ard, Christopher Kirk, and IB Terry for your support in helping get things moving, not to mention the many lessons we learned from each other in the field. To that extent, I would like to thank Microsoft DART for the opportunity to have learned the many concepts you see here. Working as part of "The Ghostbusters" for 7½ years provided me the opportunity to learn and grow as a cybersecurity professional in ways I would not have been otherwise afforded.

I would like to thank Gabriella Williams and the team at CRC Press for taking a chance on a newer author hoping to challenge the field with what I hope to be a new perspective.

I would like to thank my wife Jennifer, who has put up with the hundreds of additional hours I've spent holed up in my office or at Starbucks over the past three years. I am very glad that I was able to complete this work just in time to welcome our new daughter, Siena, into the world and look forward to spending much more time with you both going forward.

In addition, I'd like to thank my closest friends Jonathan and Austin Willman for their support and encouragement throughout this book's writing. Your confidence as well as each of your own individual drive for academic success definitely played a large part in maintaining motivation throughout this effort.

I would also like to thank John Hines for his support along the way, and for allowing me to discuss many of these concepts with your students to gauge understanding.

1

INTRODUCTION

What if I told you that all of security was fundamentally the same? Over the years, I've come to recognize a consistency that existed beneath everything – a consistency that is shared not only with technology systems but also with human processes and physical security.

I've had the opportunity to work with hundreds of customers in a variety of industries across the globe in their darkest hour as a targeted attack incident responder. At the beginning much of it felt like magic – an attacker would break into a network, move from system to system undetected, and steal or destroy at will. Today much of it feels second nature, which enables analysis of all of these systems on an equal plane – as an instantiation of just a few core concepts. In "Designing Secure Systems" I am excited to share those with you.

What Is Security?

Security is all about process. It all begins during design and development of each component and their internal and external interactions. A system deployed without security in mind will undoubtedly end up having security bolted on, which is like realizing you left a suitcase full of money in a room full of thieves. The consequence is that we end up trying to hold off the thieves while building protections rather than simply moving the money to a more secure, controlled location.

The information security market is flooded with tools which enable detection of and response to different threats. Many of these tools are necessary to provide visibility into activity within an organization, but they should not be considered solutions. Expecting a security tool to solve a vulnerability is like expecting a hammer to build a table. A carpenter is significantly more capable because of the hammer, but it is ultimately the carpenter's design and action that makes the table a reality.

Designing a secure system begins with its blueprints. The doors, windows, and building materials used in constructing a house are synonymous with a system's means of access and security tolerances. A house without a door is of little use, and one without windows is not one we would want to live in. While we could build our house with reinforced concrete walls, our budget and preferences would cause us to spend the money on a pool instead. As such, we may need to compromise a secure design for usability and to meet our budget.

Security is also dynamic. What was considered a secure solution a decade ago is probably quite vulnerable today. New platform capabilities, new attack techniques, changing business partners, changes to integrated software or systems, mergers and acquisitions, and organizational changes are just some examples of changes which may result in revisiting a system's security design.

Imagine designing the security for a castle in medieval times. A castle with thick walls, manned towers, and a moat would defend against most of the threats it would likely encounter. Today's aircraft, missiles, bombs, and tanks would bypass these medieval defenses with ease. That said, it would be a waste of time and money for a king to implement defenses against attacks that would never come to be during the castle's use.

Like the castle, the defense of any system must change occasionally based on what new threats and attacks are in use. The information security posture of any system needs to be reviewed occasionally to ensure its sufficiency. Major changes in the attack landscape such as the advent of new credential theft attacks, password spray attacks, and cryptographic weaknesses due to rising computer performance should each trigger a review of the current solution to determine its adequacy.

An effective security professional should be able to look over a system and understand the ways an attacker can use or abuse it – the ability to think like a hacker. To succeed, we need to transition from trying to make each piece of the system impenetrable to determining the impact of its loss. In other words, we need to imagine a loss of each part of the system, place ourselves in the attacker's shoes, and ask, "what can I do with what I have?"

Attackers will make it into your system regardless of how rigid security practices are. It is our goal as security professionals to design a cost-effective and usable defense based on the protected asset's value and operational impact. We must plan for an attack, ensuring that loss of a single component does not directly lead to loss of our most valued assets.

What Is a System?

A system is a set of individual components which work together to provide a capability. These components may be software, hardware, people, organizational processes, or anything else involved in a process from start to finish.

The principles behind system security have been used for hundreds of years in designing building defense, organizational processes and procedures, and in military intelligence. In cybersecurity, we adapt these concepts to the design of interconnected computers. While the platform we analyze may have changed, the principles we use to analyze these systems remain the same.

Despite its technology focus, cybersecurity follows the same set of vulnerabilities as any other system. Many of the vulnerabilities that result in compromises come from:

- Intersection of human and technology processes.
- Focus on what we believe a certain capability should do rather than what it can do.
- Misplaced trust in the security of components within a system.
- Excessive access or authorization granted for simplicity or to reduce complexity.
- Lack of security training for individuals involved in design or development of the system or its components.

As security professionals, we should assess a system both from an outsider perspective and from an assume breach mentality. When assessing a system from the outside, we look for potentially risky capabilities exposed to an untrusted source. From the assume breach perspective, we model the security of the system as if the exterior defenses failed and the attacker already has control over a part of the system.

Example: If Physical Security Was Like Technology Security

Imagine you have a large fence with barbed wire surrounding something you wish to protect. The gate to this fence is locked with a padlock. In this example, the components which make up the security perimeter are:

- The fence
- The barbed wire
- The padlock

For us to trust the security of the protected items, we must trust that the fence is durable, the barbed wire is installed correctly, and the padlock is reasonably resistant to attack.

Now, let's say you took a class on lockpicking and found that you could open the padlock rather easily without a key. At this point you're faced with three choices:

- Open and upgrade or fix the vulnerabilities in the locking mechanism to make it more difficult to pick.
- Accept that your protected asset will not be as protected as you would like.
- Buy a better lock.

Most people would choose the third option (unless perhaps you are a lock manufacturer or The Lockpicking Lawyer). This choice reflects the difference between component security and system security.

In the system security world, we must trust that individual components in the system are resilient to attack. That trust comes from our perceived reputation of the manufacturer, a needs analysis based on documentation, or sometimes certification from a third-party professional body.

Let's go back to before you picked the lock. At this moment, you may have assessed the available options of how you could get to the secured asset. You could have also:

- Used a ladder and some durable material to cover the barbed wire and climbed over the fence.
- Used a vehicle or some wire cutters to destroy the fence.
- Dug a tunnel beneath the fence.
- Used a helicopter to fast rope in from above.

Each of the possible forms of entry represents a vulnerability. One of the main jobs of a defensive security professional is to determine the value of the secured asset, the likelihood of exploitation of a known vulnerability, and the cost to secure against further attacks. The goal is to balance the cost and overhead of security measures used to protect the secured item with the value and impact of its loss.

This example demonstrates some of the challenges involved in the technology security world. Add to this the ability to access the lock from anywhere in the world and it is easy to see the challenges that manifest. Despite the difference in implementation that exists between lock design and a technology system, the underlying security design shares a number of parallels.

A Look Ahead

This book is divided into two major sections. The first section covers the concepts involved in secure system design:

- Access – the ability to interface with a system or component
- Authorization – the ability to perform the action you wish to perform with a component
- Authentication – the process of identifying an individual or system for the purpose of assessing authorization
- Vulnerability – weaknesses inherent to the system or component design which allow an attacker to circumvent intended security controls
- Impact – capabilities available to an attacker once they've attained authorization

These chapters will introduce you to the set of unified concepts which underlie all systems. We will cover each concept in-depth, with examples of each from physical, human process, and technology systems.

The second half of this book gets into the operationalization of these concepts using the NIST Cybersecurity Framework as a guide. These chapters will show you how to weaponize your new knowledge to:

- Identify sensitive information and systems
- Protect your information and systems from attack
- Detect suspicious or malicious activity within the system

- Respond to an attack, including some of the nuances involved in responding to human operated attacks
- Recover your system and restore trust in its operation

Along the way we will use a number of security standards as a means of reference, each time attempting to map the concepts to all types of systems (physical, human process, and technology). We will analyze the security of visitor check-in processes using concepts typically reserved for the technology world, perform a forensic analysis of the attack performed in the movie Oceans 11, and dig into the challenges involved with responding to human-operated attacks.

PART 1
SECURE SYSTEM CONCEPTS

2
ACCESS

Access is the ability to communicate or interact with a system or its components. Access comes in a variety of forms, such as:

- Physical: the ability to touch part of the system
- Visual: the ability to see part of the system
- Networked: the ability to route a connection to part of the system
- Radio Frequency: the ability to listen or transmit RF signals to or from part of the system
- Acoustic: the ability to hear or speak to part of the system

Access is the most basic aspect of the system, ultimately defining its capabilities and providing the potential for vulnerability. Each available form of access should supply a necessary capability to its users to justify its existence.

That said, all systems must provide some form of access. A system that provides no access may have no vulnerabilities, but also provides no value.

Capability

Each means of access defines what actions you can perform with the system. For example, an ATM enables you to withdraw money, deposit money, and sometimes transfer money between accounts. Most people wouldn't expect to be able to use an ATM to open up a new account at a bank, or to close an existing one.

A means of access provides a specific capability defined by its intended purpose. For example:

- A website provides web content for its users
- Front desk security at a building registers guests who visit a building
- A lock core in a padlock enables a user to unlock the padlock

This concept holds true as long as we can trust the security of the part providing the means of access. If an accessible component of a system is vulnerable to exploitation, an attacker may be able to manipulate the system in an unintended way.

For example, an attacker may be able to perform unintended malicious activity if the ATM's software is vulnerable to attack. The limit of what an ATM can do when exploited expands up to the maximum capability which the underlying computer can do. In this case, the attacker may be able to open or close a bank account if the system blindly trusts decisions made by the ATM.

Using our previous examples:

- A website running vulnerable code can enable an attacker to remotely control the system or its database.
- A social engineer can trick the front desk security agent into performing reconnaissance for them.
- An attacker can gain illegitimate access to our secured item without a key if our padlock can be disassembled without being unlocked.

From a system security perspective, we must be able to trust that parts of the system which provide access are secure. Without this trust the entire concept of system security falls apart. That said, we must also design the system to accommodate for an unknown vulnerability in a means of access by limiting its capability based on its exposure to risk. The more exposed a means of access, the less we should trust its decisions and the less we should enable it to do.

For example, we can:

- Validate activity performed by an ATM on the server side before performing any action and alert when abnormal activity occurs.
- Reduce what our webserver has access to and use credentials that are not valid elsewhere in the system.
- Limit the information available to the front desk agent to what is necessary for their role in the organization.
- Limit the value of items secured by a presumed vulnerable padlock (or replace the lock with a more trusted one).

Directionality

Directionality describes the way communication occurs over a means of access. There are three types of directionality that a means of access can have: send, receive, and bidirectional.

Many forms of access are bidirectional – meaning that they can both send and receive a signal. For example, most networked devices provide bidirectional communication capabilities. These means of access are convenient in that the architect needs to expose only a single means of access to allow users to send or receive information from the system.

Bidirectional access is also convenient for an attacker since it allows a single communication channel to provide both control over a compromised component and the ability to receive the results from their commands. For example, an attacker could use a walkie-talkie to both listen in on a conversation and participate in it.

Other forms of access only allow sending or receiving of information. For example, radio stations use powerful broadcast towers to transmit a signal, while a car radio is only useful for receiving a signal (note that this is not necessarily true for streaming services and other network-connected radios).

The directionality of access defines the available capabilities and potential vulnerabilities a form of access may have. In our radio example, it would be unlikely that an attacker would be able to manipulate the broadcast equipment by sending a signal into the antenna since it is an outbound medium. That said, if the signal being transmitted by the radio tower is strong enough the attacker may be able to listen in if they are within range.

Just the same, an attacker would probably be unable to listen in on conversations happening within a car through its radio antenna since it only receives information. They could, however, overpower the signal from the radio tower to either jam it or replace it with their own content.

Indirect Access

How access occurs within a system is not always straightforward. Sometimes systems use a form of indirect access to provide its capability. An attacker may also choose to use indirect access to accommodate for limitations in a system or to obfuscate their operations. There are three different general methods that can be used for this purpose: direct access, proxy access, or asymmetric access.

Direct Access

The simplest form of access is direct access. In direct access, the client accesses the target resource without any other resources in the middle. Direct access is what most people think of when approaching this topic.

Proxy Access

Proxy access occurs when access to a resource occurs through another resource. Let's use a physical world example to describe how proxy access works.

Imagine you have just left work for the day and are driving home when suddenly you realize that you left a piece of paper you needed on your desk. You currently have no direct access to the piece of paper but need the phone number written on it. Instead of driving all the way back to work, you might decide to call the person who sits in a nearby desk and ask them to read the phone number to you.

In this scenario, you were able to gain access to the paper by calling a coworker. The coworker had physical access to the paper, enabling them to read the number and provide it to you. You used your ability to access your coworker over the phone and joined that with their ability to access the paper on your desk to get access to the phone number.

Proxy access occurs in a variety of applications, including:

- Multitier websites
- When a company representative performs actions on your behalf (such as a bank teller, your phone company representative, etc.)

- When you call a function in a program and it performs an action on your behalf that you wouldn't be able to perform directly

Attackers frequently use proxy access to pivot within a network. The first system compromised by an attacker is usually not the ultimate target of the operation, but it gets them closer to their target. To gain access to other systems, the attacker will typically install malware on this compromised host and use it to access resources that would otherwise be inaccessible. These newly accessible resources are then accessed by the attacker by proxying the connection through the initially compromised host.

Asymmetric Access

Sometimes control and data communications occur over two separate channels. To visualize this, let's imagine you are contacting your phone company for a copy of your last bill.

In this scenario, you may begin by calling the phone company on your phone. Since the representative is not likely to read your entire bill over the phone, they will probably send a copy via email. In this case, the control channel (requesting a copy of your bill) occurred over a cell phone, while the data channel (the copy of your bill) occurred over email.

In technology, asymmetric access is frequently used in report generation. A report is a summary of a larger dataset which may involve multiple accounts, customers, or other facets. The application generating the report typically has access to all of this information and generates a summary on the user's behalf. Once complete, the summarized report is provided in a location where the user can access it. In this model, the user proxies their request through the application to the back-end database and gets the data over a separate channel (the report).

Attackers sometimes use asymmetric access to covertly export data to a public location. For example, an attacker may use a vulnerability in a website to trick the application into exporting all customer data and send it to a cloud storage service. This enables them to hide their control channel and provides high-speed access to the results without giving away their network information.

Access and Layers

A single form of access can be described in different ways depending on the level of granularity we need. For example, a network connection can be described as:

- Two applications communicating with each other
- A data connection between two IP addresses
- An interconnection of a series of routers between the source and destination
- The physical path between all of the switches, routers, and other networking devices used to connect the two systems

Each of these layers describes a different set of means of access, each with their own potential vulnerabilities. For example, to describe a physical wiretap, we would need to know the specific cable where the wiretap was installed. If we wanted to describe a vulnerability in how the application handles a connection, we would be looking at the application layer. For port mirroring or other network-based attacks, we would likely need to describe the means of access at either the routing or switching layer depending on where the port mirror occurred.

The important aspect about access and layers is keeping in mind that protection applied at one layer does not always mean that everything above or below that layer of access is secure. To demonstrate this, imagine you wanted to secure the route into a city and only allow approved individuals to pass. You could install a large wall around the city and post guards at its entrance, but this only partially solves the issue – a person could use a helicopter to fly over the wall, a properly equipped person could climb the wall, or perhaps even tunnel under the wall. While the wall is likely to deter the majority of people from entering the city, we would need to address the problem at a higher layer (ways to enter the city) to properly measure security.

The layer problem is more prevalent in technology due to the number of layers that can exist. Imagine we now want to secure inbound network traffic to a server. One solution might be to install a firewall on the edge and explicitly define network routes that can be used to access the server. The problem is the need to know every path that someone can take to bypass the firewall. For example, an attacker might:

- Use stolen VPN credentials to tunnel through the firewall.
- Compromise another endpoint that can route to the server and proxy their access.
- Socially engineer someone who can connect to the server to perform the action on their behalf.
- Fake source network information to make the firewall think we are coming from a trusted source.

Each of these routes are possible ways that an attacker can gain access to the server despite the firewall being installed.

3
AUTHORIZATION

Authorization is a security control that can be used to limit which actions are allowed to be performed based on identity. In other words, access determines which operations are capable, whereas authorization decides which of the actions an identity is allowed to perform.

For example, a person can go to a bank and perform deposits, withdrawals, open or close accounts, and so on. The ability to perform these actions on a given account is determined on the basis of a list of authorized users for the account. The bank representative will ask the person which account they wish to use, then ask for identification to authenticate them, and last compare their identity to a list of individuals who may use the account. In this example, the bank teller is acting as the authorization control mechanism which determines whether the requested action is allowed.

Authorization cannot exist without access. For example, you might know that a lock is easy to pick if you know the model from looking at it, but it won't do any good if you can't physically get to the lock. That said, you might be incentivized to find a way to get physical access to that lock if you know that the lock protects a valuable asset and can be picked.

This is no different in the technology world. In old school systems design, the solution to a potential security vulnerability was always to put a firewall in front of it. The firewall would limit access, thereby preventing an attacker from abusing the capability. This approach also enabled system designers to take a more lax approach at designing authorization control since an attacker can't very well abuse something that was made inaccessible to them.

Today the world is highly interconnected and the inability to access a resource may be more costly than defending it. Movements such as cloud, Bring Your Own Device (BYOD), and Internet of Things (IoT) are behind the push from an access-based security model to an authorization-based one. Anymore, it is almost an expectation that any resource should be accessible from just about any device.

Fundamentals of Authorization

The beginning of an authorization control system is identifying the entity that is trying to perform an action. This determination is made through authentication, the process of identifying a principal using credentials. We will cover authentication in the next chapter, but for the purposes of discussion, a successful authentication will result in an authenticated entity attempting to perform an action over a means of access.

Authorization control is used everywhere in both the physical and virtual world. Some common examples of authorization controls include:

- A bank teller validating your identity before performing a withdrawal
- A gate representative checking your ticket before gaining access to an event
- Scanning your employee badge to unlock a door
- An email system authenticating users to provide access to their emails

Trust in the system and its components is required for authorization to work properly. Lack of trust in any part of the system performing authorization control can lead to abuse of the system. For example:

- The bank teller could modify other people's accounts or mishandle money.
- The gate representative could let their friends through without a ticket.
- An improperly configured door security system may allow people access to unnecessary rooms.
- The email system could have a vulnerability which enables an attacker to gain illegitimate authorization to a mailbox.

Always perform a full security review when a service transitions from access control to authorization control. Use of an access control may have hidden poor security practices such as vulnerable components or lax access control lists. Simply providing access to a service without review may inadvertently introduce vulnerability in your system, ultimately leading to compromise.

Principles of Authorization

Authorization control can be broken into five components:

- Domains
- Principals
- Securables
- Trusts
- Membership

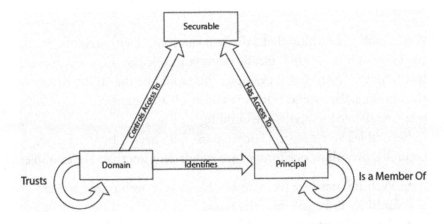

Domains

A domain is the part of the authorization control system which authenticates principals and controls access to securables. A domain is the "security guard" in an authorization control system who validates the identity of people and ensures that they're allowed to access the building.

For an authorization control system to be successful, we need to be able to trust the integrity of the domain's decisions. In other words, we couldn't trust decisions made by the security guard if they accept bribery to let unauthorized individuals through, or if they secretly worked as a spy for a competitor.

Principals

A principal is any identity that can be granted access to something secured by a domain. Using our security guard example, the people accessing the building would each be principals. A principal doesn't have to always be a person. For example, if a package is delivered to the organization the security guard may allow the package to enter, but not the delivery person.

Principals are the entities in an authorization control system which we authenticate. Our trust in the identity of a principal is only as good as our means of authentication. For example, we can't trust the identity of individuals if our security guard accepts handwritten notes with the person's name on them as proof of their identity.

Securables

A securable is anything that a domain can control authorization to. In the IT world, these are typically items controlled by an access control list. In our security guard example, this would be the ability to access the building. The guard is likely to have a list of approved individuals who are allowed to access the building.

Securables aren't always simple pass–fail checks. In some cases, a securable may allow one form of access but deny another. For example:

- Website users are likely to be able to read web pages, but are unlikely to be able to write them.
- An application may be able to read or write files or memory within its context, but it may not be allowed to read or write to system memory or files.
- A person may be able to access the building, but they may not necessarily have access to every door within it.

Groups and Membership

Granting authorization to individual principals only works when very few principals have authorization. Role-based access control enables you to use groups to assign authorization to groups of principals. These groups may represent company employees, specific teams within the company, or other standardized set of permissions granted to a set of principals.

Some systems also enable recursive group membership, which means you can place groups inside of groups. While this simplifies delegation, it can also make determining exactly which principals have a given authorization difficult. For example, an IT professional may accidentally grant excessive permissions to many users by not realizing the number of members a group has.

Trust

A trust is a condition whereby one domain delegates the authentication of a set of principals to another domain. Trusts enable an organization to scale and simplify the management of credentials by using a single set of credentials to authenticate a principal to multiple components of a system.

While using a trust simplifies design, it also delegates critical security decisions outside of that part of the system. In other words, a breach of a trusted domain may directly lead to a breach of the trusting domain.

For example, let's say we're a security guard back at our secure office facility. Your manager approaches the security desk with a person whom they identify as a business partner. In most cases, you are likely to accept that the person your manager is escorting is a business partner because you trust their authentication.

Now let's imagine your manager is not trustworthy, but instead was secretly a spy for a competitor. Your manager might be escorting malicious individuals into the organization and you wouldn't know any better. Trusts provide simplicity and scalability at the cost of confidence in authenticity.

User and Administrative Authorization

Authorization comes in two generic categories: user or administrative. User authorization, as the name implies, enables a principal to use the system. Depending on the system, this could mean having the ability to:

- Open a padlock with a key
- Open a door with an ID card

- Read and write to data files in data directories throughout the system
- Download that identity's mail items from a mail server

Administrative authorization grants the principal the ability to manipulate the authorization process itself. This authorization is significantly more impactful to system security because it enables the principal to compromise trust in the authorization control system itself. Using our earlier examples, administrative control could mean having the ability to:

- Add or change the keys that worked with a padlock
- Configure which ID cards could open which doors
- Write to files in sensitive system locations or read from protected system memory
- Change access control lists on the mail server or download mail items from any user's mailbox

A principal with administrative authorization can undermine the trust in the authorization control system, meaning that a compromise of a principal with administrative authorization can lead to loss in trust in the overall system. As a result, principals granted administrative authorization should be closely guarded and limited in number.

Least Privilege

The principle of least privilege dictates that a principal should be granted the least amount of authorization necessary to fulfill its purpose. In other words, if a principal only needs the ability to read a file there is no reason to grant it the ability to write to the file.

There is a balance between granting excessive authorization and incurring too much administrative overhead by tailoring authorization too granularly. For example, in many cases controlling authorization at a file level is unnecessary and will result in excessive overhead as administrators change access control lists constantly for each principal that needs access. Instead, it is much more effective to place all files with similar authorization requirements in the same folder and control authorization at the folder level or at the server level.

At its core, the goal of least privilege design is to avoid granting unnecessary access or authorization as a general practice. The balance in granularity will be different for each system depending on its purpose, impact, and sensitivity.

Authorization and Relativity

All authorization is measured relative to something. In other words, saying that a principal has read authorization doesn't mean anything unless you specify what the principal has read authorization to. Authorization can only be granted to securables, therefore in many cases, you can say you have read access to a file, share, or the document sitting on your coworker's desk unsecured.

Sometimes measuring access relative to the specific securable is insufficient to determine potential impact. For example, imagine if the document on your coworker's desk had all the administrative passwords for the organization. The impact of having read access to that document differs significantly from if it were a prerelease quarterly earnings report or a simple menu of what the cafeteria plans to serve for lunch. In each of these scenarios, you had read access to a document, but the impact of that read access changed dramatically based on its contents.

In our administrative password example, the impact was not only relative to the document but also relative to every system whose administrative password was on the list. From a systems perspective, your coworker was trusted to protect the confidentiality of these credentials. They delegated the ability to read the file to everyone who could access their desk, thus granting authorization by proxy to anyone who could access their desk.

In the software world, this occurs when a process writes sensitive information to a user readable location and is called an information leak or information disclosure vulnerability. An attacker can exploit these vulnerabilities to gain sensitive information that they would otherwise not have access to.

In the systems world, this can occur when sensitive authorization is trusted to an untrustworthy domain. For example, imagine we granted administrative authorization to a domain with lax security practices and policies. Their poor security practices may result in compromise of their systems, which, in turn, may compromise yours.

Cryptography

Most authorization-based security only works when the system is available to determine whether a principal can perform a requested action. That said, there are many conditions whereby data or control needs protection while the system is offline or unable to perform authorization decisions. For these situations, cryptography can protect the confidentiality of sensitive information or detect attempts to tamper with integrity.

Cryptography can ensure the confidentiality, integrity, or authenticity of data or control without needing to directly communicate with a service. This makes cryptography ideal for protecting against offline attacks or while data are in-transit between the two systems.

Hashing

Hash functions convert a variable sized input to a fixed size output. File hashes are used for comparing the similarity of data without needing to send the actual data itself.

Hashing algorithms come in two forms with very distinct purposes. The most common use of hashing algorithms, called cryptographic hashing, uses a fixed-length value to uniquely represent the exact contents of the data.

Cryptographic Hashing   In a cryptographic hash, any slight change to the contents of the data should produce a totally different hash value. In a good hash algorithm, there should be no way to determine the contents of the data from the hash value aside from brute force. This means that hash values can be transmitted freely without significant concern for the confidentiality of the file contents.

Common uses of cryptographic hashes include:

- File-based malware research
- Validation of data integrity
- Creation of unique identifiers for data within a database
- Protection of credentials during authentication

Fuzzy Hashing   Fuzzy hash algorithms work in the opposite way of cryptographic hashes. Fuzzy hash algorithms compare the level of similarity between two files. In a fuzzy hash algorithm, highly similar data inputs are likely to produce either the same or a highly similar result.

Fuzzy hashes are useful in a variety of ways, including:

- Detecting attempts to dodge cryptographic hash-based file research (called polymorphism)
- Clustering together highly similar data
- Detection of plagiarism
- Search algorithms

Encryption

Encryption algorithms protect the confidentiality of data using keys. Encryption is a form of authorization control because encrypted information is unreadable without the associated decryption key, which acts as a form of authentication.

Encrypted data can be limited to a specific audience based on a credential; therefore, it works in the same way as an access control list in software. This holds true as long as only intended parties have the decryption key, just the same as with credentials in authentication.

Encryption is used to protect data both in-transit and at rest. Some examples of encryption include:

- Secure sockets layer (SSL)
- Transport layer security (TLS)
- Virtual private networking (VPN)
- Hard drive encryption
- Password protected zip files

Digital Signature

Digital signatures are a combination of a cryptographic hash and an encryption algorithm which can prove both the integrity of the data being signed and the identity of the signer. Together this establishes authenticity since we can prove the data hasn't changed and that the signature must've been created by someone who has the encryption key.

While a digital signature may not be able to prevent write access to data, it can be used to detect modifications made by unauthorized individuals. Any change to the signed data will cause the cryptographic hash to no longer match, thus indicating that the data have been tampered with. We can also identify whether the modification was made by someone we trust based on whether we are able to decrypt the hash using the associated key.

Digital signatures are used in authentication, software development, and documents. Some examples of digital signatures include:

- Electronically signed documents
- Kerberos authentication
- Authenticode code signing
- Public key infrastructure (PKI) certificates

4

AUTHENTICATION

Authentication is the process of identifying a principal using credentials. A credential is one or more values, tokens, or attributes that we attribute to the principal. The more confidence we have that the principal is the only one that has the credential, the more we can trust our confidence in their identity.

Credentials can be a variety of things, such as:

- A password
- A physical key
- An identity card issued by a trusted organization
- A physical attribute of the principal
- A security token issued by the organization
- A picture

The Authentication Process

Authentication occurs when a credential is used to identify something or someone, typically in the process of granting authorization to perform an action. Let's take a look at the concepts of authentication and how they are related to authorization.

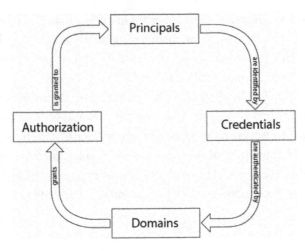

Authentication involves four concepts: Principals, Credentials, Domains, and Authorization. These concepts work together to enable an authorization-based system to make decisions.

In our padlock example, the credential is the physical key that corresponds with the tumblers on the lock. The lock identifies the person (the principal) attempting to unlock the padlock (the domain) based on their possession of a key (the credential), which matches the pattern encoded in its tumblers. If this all works correctly, the person can unlock the padlock (the requested authorization) and gain access to whatever it protects. We can trust the security of items protected by the padlock as long as only approved individuals have the key and if we're not concerned with anyone picking the lock.

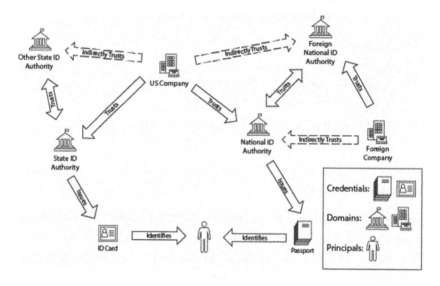

Another common example of authentication happens whenever we use a form of government identification, such as a driver's license or passport. In the picture above, the individual (our principal) has two different credentials – a state ID card and a passport.

Let's say the individual needs to authenticate themselves to a company within their own state. Our principal should be able to use either credential if a government ID is enough to identify them to the organization. If our principal were from another state, the company would still likely accept the ID card because the organization trusts the state ID authority, and that authority trusts other state ID authorities transitively. Just the same, our principal could likely use a passport issued from a foreign country because the organization trusts the federal government, which in turn trusts other passport authorities.

Now imagine our principal jumps on a plane and travels to a foreign country. These foreign countries are unlikely to trust their state ID card for identification; therefore, they would need to use their passport to prove their identity.

The Value of a Credential

Credentials can be incredibly valuable assets. A single username and password combination may be the only line of defense protecting your organization's most sensitive data and systems from an attacker. But credentials are not all equally valuable. For example, a system administrator's credentials or a company's Authenticode signing certificate is a lot more valuable than the credentials of an individual contributor in a call center.

$$Credential\ Value = \left(\sum_{Service} Authorization \right) \times Validity\ Period$$

The value of a credential is derived from three concepts: the number of places it is accepted, the level of authorization granted at each place it is accepted, and its validity period. This formula can be used to compare the value of credentials and determine necessary protections to help limit their exposure, or provide justification for redesign of the authentication system to reduce the value of credentials, thereby reducing risk.

Notice that we are measuring distinct authorizations. A credential that provides multiple ways to gain a specific authorization is no more valuable than if it only provided a single way to gain that authorization. For example, the key to your house doesn't increase in value based on the number of locked doors you put on your house (if it's the same key everywhere).

The second factor is the validity period of the credential. Credentials with a longer validity period are significantly more valuable than those with a short validity period. A stolen credential with a long validity period, such as a website certificate, has the potential to provide value for a much longer period of time than say a session cookie that may only be valid for few minutes.

While subjective, this formula enables us to measure all credentials equally. Let's look at some real-world examples where we can apply this calculation.

Valuing a Physical Key

In our key and padlock example, our key enables the owner to open the padlock. We can determine the value of opening the padlock based on what it secures. The value of this operation is quite different if the padlock is on a janitor's closet versus on a cabinet holding sensitive documents.

Now imagine if we can use the same key to open multiple padlocks throughout the organization. Suddenly, the key becomes more valuable – and its value is based on the maximum potential impact of its loss. If this key opens ten janitorial closets throughout the company it's not a big deal; however, if it also opens a lock protecting an organization's research and development lab it suddenly becomes quite valuable.

While we are on the topic, imagine that the key opened two doors to the same space. While these are two separate locks, the resulting authorization of opening both is the same – you gain access to the same space.

A physical key has an infinite validity period – it stays valid until the locks are rekeyed (thus changing the shared secret) or replaced. This means that our stolen key can be immensely valuable if it protects highly valuable assets. That said, remember that the attacker would need to access the padlock to use the key. This means that the key may be a reasonable secondary form of protection if another layer of security protects the space itself.

Valuing Personal Credentials

Personal security includes websites you log on to regularly such as your bank account, social media, or personal email. Credentials used for personal security typically fall into two one of two categories:

individually authenticated websites and those that use federated authentication (such as Facebook, Google, or Microsoft accounts).

The value of a credential in federated authentication can be determined on the basis of the value of the information available at sites authenticated by the credential. If you use your Facebook login to authenticate to your personal blog, collaboration service, or shipping company then the credential's potential authorization is the total capabilities that it provides.

In the other case, where you need to log on separately to each website, the value of the credential depends on how many places you share the same username and password. For example, if you use the same username and password to access your bank, investments, and personal email the total would be the sum value of those authorizations.

The validity period of a credential in personal security is typically going to be based on how often you change your password. Most sites designed for individual users don't force you to change your password periodically; therefore, the validity period could be indefinite.

Credential Exposure

A credential's exposure is a list of places where it is available to be read in a reusable fashion. Exposed credentials can enable an attacker to reuse the identity associated with the credential, providing them with any authorization granted to the principal.

While credential exposure sounds simple, it is not always a straightforward measurement. Some forms of credential exposure include:

- Saving a credential to a file
- Reusing the same credential with different domains
- Storing the credential in user-accessible memory
- Entering the credential into a compromised system
- Watching a user enter their password using a camera
- Sending a credential over an unencrypted network connection
- Sharing a credential between multiple users

Each of these situations provides additional opportunities for an attacker to steal a reusable credential, thereby enabling them to masquerade as the principal to any systems where it is accepted.

In our personal security example, we used the same credential for different websites and services. Because of this, a compromise of any one of the websites indirectly leads to a compromise of all the web-sites. Attackers commonly sell information stolen from cyberattacks on the dark web (a set of hidden non-attributable websites tunneled within the Internet), which means a single breach may provide mul-tiple attackers with all information associated with the credential at all of the locations where it is valid.

Credential Value and Exposure in Enterprise IT

Many enterprise IT organizations struggle with managing high value credentials and credential exposure. Today, many organizations man-age their own authentication system in-house. These systems are not always as well-protected as the big-name authentication providers which are under constant attack.

Administrative authorization is loosely controlled in many enter-prise environments. Many IT professionals and software developers have a bad habit of granting accounts admin authorization rather than troubleshooting to determine the appropriate permissions. This is also a problem with software vendors that tell customers to simply grant application identities administrative authorization instead of figuring out the actual permissions needed for their application.

Enterprise IT also struggles with credential exposure. Despite training, users tend to share passwords between their personal and company user accounts. This means that a breach of a public website can indirectly lead to compromise of their organization's credentials.

Partners also pose a risk to enterprise IT organizations. Many organizations provide accounts to enable their partners to collaborate on business objectives or interact with proprietary internal systems. These credentials are usually sent to partners over email, which means anyone with the ability to read the email can masquerade as the part-ner's identity.

Another risk associated with business partnerships occurs when a partner is breached. Breach of a business partner's systems could mean:

- Any credentials shared with the partner network may be exposed to the attacker.
- Any identities authenticated by a domain from the partner network may be compromised.

- Bad practices around handling credentials within the partner network may indirectly lead to a compromise of your organization.

Multifactor Authentication

Multifactor authentication, or MFA, is a process where multiple individual credentials are used to identify a principal. MFA makes credential theft more difficult for an attacker by requiring the principal to use credentials from two or more of the following categories:

- Something you know, such as a password
- Something you have, such as a cell phone, hardware token, or ID badge
- Something you are, such as a fingerprint, retina scan, or facial recognition

MFA helps secure initial authentication to a service but does not work for every authentication throughout the system. For example, imagine if you had to enter your password and fingerprint each time you clicked a link on a website. This approach is impractical; therefore, most services use a process called credential translation to convert the initial MFA authentication into a new simpler credential used to authenticate the principal throughout their session. We will cover credential translation shortly.

Attributes of a Credential

Credentials have several attributes which identify the associated principal, describe their purpose, and describe their issuer. The attributes associated with a credential will differ depending on the credential's purpose, the system's capabilities, and security requirements.

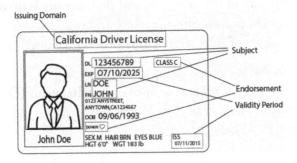

Secret

The secret in a credential is the portion which validates the identity of its associated principal. A domain compares the secret to an expected value during authentication to validate the identity of the principal.

The strength of a credential is based on the difficulty of discovering or replicating the secret. For example, in password authentication systems the strength is determined by the length and complexity of the password. In an ID card, anti-tamper mechanisms and complex designs make the credential more difficult to reproduce or tamper with.

For authentication to work, the secret must be usable by the principal and able to be validated by the domain. To accomplish this, the secret needs to be known or able to be derived by the domain.

Some examples of secrets include:

- A password associated with a user account
- The pattern of a government ID
- The pattern of a physical key
- The private key to a certificate
- An encryption key

Subject

The subject of a credential identifies the principal being authenticated. Without a subject, a credential can only be used to provide a basic pass\fail determination.

Our padlock is an example of a credential without a subject. The padlock will open for anyone who has the corresponding key but has no concept of who is using the key. In contrast, our ID card example proves the identity of the principal, and that identity is used to determine whether the person can enter the building.

Some examples of subjects in authentication include:

- A username specified during authentication
- A photograph or other descriptive attribute on an ID card
- The subject value of an SSL certificate
- An e-mail address

Endorsements

Endorsements are permissions, qualities, aliases, or other information certified by the domain that created the credential. For example,
a driver's license may state that the driver is also allowed to ride a
motorcycle or drive a commercial vehicle.

In enterprise authentication, endorsements are used to identify
group membership. This enables clients to determine a principal's
group membership during authorization checks without repetitive
calls back to the server.

Restrictions

A restriction is the opposite of an endorsement – it specifies limitations for a credential based on its use. Restrictions are important when
a credential's authorization is determined by a trusted domain.

For example, a driver's license may specify that the driver needs
to wear glasses when driving their car. This means that despite the
driver's license being a valid credential to drive a car, it is only valid
for that purpose if they are wearing glasses.

Issuing Domain

We use issuing domains with authentication trusts to enable the
authenticating domain to know where the principal's account or registration exists. For example, your government ID card will list the
state where your information is registered.

Credentials need to specify which domain issued a credential to
enable the authenticating domain to know where to validate the secret.
For example, in password authentication, the authenticating domain
keeps a database of users and their valid password (hopefully a hash
or encrypted version of their password and not the password itself).

When a trusting domain receives an authentication request from
a user in a trusted domain, it may send the credential to the issuing
domain to determine its validity. The issuing domain then validates
the credential and responds with the result.

The issuing domain field also helps an authenticating domain determine whether they trust the credential's issuer. One example of this

occurs when a web browser validates an SSL certificate. During validation, the browser checks the issuing domain of the certificate to see if it chains to a certificate authority it trusts. If the certificate's issuer chains to an unknown authority, the certificate is deemed invalid.

Validity Period

A credential's validity period specifies the timeframe during which it should be considered valid. A validity period reduces the impact of credential theft by requiring the principal to obtain a new credential periodically. This limits the value of a credential to an attacker and improves the system's confidence in the authenticity of its principals.

Using our ID card example, the validity period would be the issue and expiration dates. Anyone validating the identity of the holder should ensure that the current date is within that range.

Where possible, a credential's validity should be less time than it would take an attacker to guess its secret through brute force.

Revocation Information

Revocation is the process of invalidating a credential while it is still within its validity period. Revocation information is especially important if a credential has a longer validity period due to the potential impact of its loss.

For example, the DMV may revoke a driver's license within its validity period if the driver is irresponsible. The police officer has a system that determines whether the license is revoked, and therefore whether it is a valid credential despite being within its validity period.

One common credential that typically includes revocation information is PKI certificates, in large part due to their typically long validity period and potential impact of compromise. For example, your web browser may check the revocation status of an SSL certificate when you visit an encrypted website.

Credential Translation

Credential translation occurs whenever a system authenticates a principal and provides it with a different credential for use when communicating with the system. Some common examples of credential translation include:

- A webserver authenticating a user and providing them a session cookie
- A security guard validating your identity and giving you a badge that allows you to access the building
- Using your government ID and birth certificate to obtain a passport

Let's take a look at a few different cases where a system uses credential translation and the reasons why.

Performance

Sometimes the process used for initial authentication can be time-consuming or computationally intensive. Authentication using strong keys can be costly to performance if the principal will be communicating with the system frequently. Therefore, the system may convert the stronger initial credential into a faster session-specific credential.

One example of this occurs in SSL encryption. In SSL, the webserver authenticates itself to the client using a strong certificate-based system. This initial authentication can be time-consuming, involving multiple external services as the client checks each certificate in the webserver's CA chain and its revocation status.

Rather than performing this action repeatedly each time a user accesses a different page on the website, the client generates a session-specific encryption key and encrypts it with the server's certificate credential for use during their session. This key provides faster encrypted communication and is reliably secure as long as the session key is only known to the client and the webserver.

Differing Credentials

Another example of credential translation occurs when the system you are planning to access cannot accept the type of credential you have. In our building visitor badge example, you proved your identity to a security guard to obtain a visitor badge to the facility. One of the reasons this is necessary is that your original form if authentication (either your driver's license or passport) would probably not be accepted by doors and other security controls within the facility.

In technology, sometimes the service you need to access cannot accept the credential type that you have. For example, you may use a smart card or certificate to authenticate to a gateway which then uses a different form of credential to authenticate you to a back-end system. This type of translation is common with delegation – where a system can authenticate a user on their behalf.

Differing Authorization

Sometimes a system translates a credential to provide it different authorization. This occurs when a domain needs to specify authorization or membership which may not be specified on the original credential.

Let's go back to our visitor badge example again. The visitor badge is a credential which provides you authorization to the building. Employees of secure organizations are trained to watch for people without visitor badges to help prevent unauthorized entry. Although your government ID may prove your identity to anyone in the building, it doesn't tell them that you're authorized to be there. Therefore, the visitor badge displays your authorization to walk through the building.

Some software systems, such as single sign-on applications, use a similar concept to convey a principal's membership or authorization. This improves the performance of authorization checks by software by preventing them from having to repeat the process of determining the principal's membership or authorization.

Account Provisioning

In account provisioning, authentication is used to create a new set of credentials within a domain. The new credentials typically are for a different purpose from the original credentials.

Let's use our passport example to describe account provisioning in the physical world. When you initially apply for a passport you need to prove your identity, residence, and citizenship. Once proved, those individual authentications result in them providing you with a new "account" with the nation's passport organization and a new credential – your passport.

Account provisioning occurs the first time you use a system in the technology world. These accounts may be created by an administrator of the system or automatically if an authorization is not needed during account creation. For example, free online services usually let anyone create an account if they confirm their ownership of an email address or phone number. In contrast, corporate information systems typically need you to prove that you are either an employee or a partner before creating a user account.

Risks of Credential Translation

Credential translation is a sensitive process that has several risks associated with it. Errors in credential translation may enable an attacker to use an illegitimate account or increase their authorization. Let's look at some of the checks that should be performed during the credential translation process.

Revocation Status

The revocation status of a translated credential should be aligned with the revocation status of the original credential where appropriate. This enables the organization to recall all credentials associated with the principal in the event of a compromise. If the revocation status of the translated credential is not tied to the initial credential, the principal may still be able to use the translated identity despite revocation of the initial account.

For example, imagine you work at an organization that has multiple accounts per user. If you needed to terminate an employee it is important to ensure all of their accounts are invalidated during their termination, otherwise they may still be able to authenticate to the organization's services. If that employee had the ability to create accounts on behalf of the organization, they may have created a backdoor account which enables them to maintain control.

This concern highlights an identity management issue within many organizations. To avoid this, the validity status of all accounts throughout the system should be controlled by a single source of truth where possible. Using a central source simplifies auditing of accounts throughout the organization and reduces the likelihood of backdoor accounts. If possible, all credentials created by an identity should be revalidated if the identity which created the credential is revoked.

Note that we are discussing revoked credentials and not expired credentials in this section. A revoked credential implies that the credential is compromised and therefore must be terminated prematurely, whereas an expired credential is simply one where its validity has run out. Expired credentials are therefore less concerning from a security perspective and may not need as rigid of an approach.

Some credentials need their revocation status to be tied to the validity of their original credentials. If the translated credential is meant to be a representation of a session tied to the user's logon you may want to invalidate the credential if the credentials from the original logon change.

Imagine you have a web application that lets users remember their browser to prevent them from having to log on each time. If the user feels their account is compromised, they may change their credentials to prevent any new sessions from being created using the compromised credentials. This action should invalidate any sessions based on the original credential to maintain control.

Validity Period

An identity translated from another credential should have a validity period that is within the original credential's validity period. This practice prevents a translated credential from existing when its parent identity is no longer considered valid.

For example, imagine your company is bringing in temporary workers for a period of 90 days to do some work within the organization. For security purposes, all credentials issued to the temporary workers should expire within that 90-day period to ensure they do not have authorization after their job is complete. If their contract is renewed or they are hired full-time, a new authentication should occur to extend their credentials to the new expiration date.

Full-time employees of an organization should have some period whereby their accounts are renewed to ensure that an oversight in account management doesn't result in a credential existing forever.

In software, we should always ensure that session tokens are not issued for a longer period than the initial authentication credential. Using our saved browser example, the saved browser session should not be valid for a longer period than the credential that created it (if the credential that created it has an expiration).

Credential Types

A credential is either symmetric or asymmetric depending on how validation occurs. The difference between symmetric and asymmetric credentials is the type of secret associated with the credential. Let's take a look at how symmetric and asymmetric credentials are used and the benefits and drawbacks to each.

Symmetric Credentials

A symmetric credential is one where the authentication or encryption process uses the same key to both encrypt and decrypt data, or to identify a principal. Symmetric operations are typically much faster and simpler than asymmetric operations, thus they are the more common.

Everyone involved in encryption, decryption, or authentication needs to have a copy of the credential or a mathematically symmetrical representation thereof. For example, a password authentication system only works if the system you are authenticating to can validate that the correct password was entered for the principal. This can occur if:

- The authentication system knows the cleartext password
- The authentication system has an encrypted copy of the password, or
- The authentication system has a hashed version of the password

The nature of symmetric credentials can cause problems with key distribution. For example, if you wanted to have individual sessions with 100 different principals you would require 100 different credentials. If all 100 principals wanted to authenticate to each other in a mesh fashion, you would require $100 \times (100 - 1)/2$, or 4,950 different credentials.

Some symmetric authentication systems reduce this complexity through centralization and trust. For example, directory services and single sign-on systems can authenticate users on behalf of an application, thereby reducing the number of places where passwords are stored.

Credential exposure can be a problem when using a symmetric authentication system with single sign-on, given that credentials may be exposed to a system requesting authentication despite the authentication occurring on a different trusted server. If the system requesting authentication is compromised, the attacker may be able to read the credential in memory or from network communication.

Some examples of symmetric credentials include:

- Passwords
- Physical keys
- The design of an ID card
- A biometric attribute
- Data written on the magnetic stripe on a credit card
- Kerberos authentication

Asymmetric Credentials

Asymmetric credentials use two mathematically related keys to authenticate a principal. Data encrypted by one key can only be decrypted by its corresponding paired key and not by the same key that encrypted it. This provides a strong defense against credential theft since the value of an individual key in the pair is half that of a symmetric credential.

Math behind asymmetric credentials is significantly more complex than that of symmetric credentials, thus making it less efficient for frequent use. They are also not suited for human authentication since the math and keys involved in asymmetric cryptography tend to be quite difficult.

The benefit of asymmetric credentials is that they do not suffer the same key distribution issues of symmetric credentials. In most cases, one of the keys in an asymmetric pair is distributed broadly as a means of providing secure communication with the principals that have the corresponding key. This model also enables strong authentication of the principal since any data encrypted by its key can only be decrypted by its corresponding pair.

Some common examples of asymmetric cryptography include:

- Certificates
- PGP encryption
- Smart card authentication
- SSL encryption
- S/MIME encrypted and signed e-mails

Combining the Technologies

The real benefit of these technologies comes when they are combined. One way to accomplish this is by using asymmetric credentials for initial authentication, then using a symmetric credential throughout the session.

Using an asymmetric credential for initial authentication provides strong authentication and limits the exposure of reusable credentials. The reusable portion of the credential can be kept solely with the principal being authenticated; therefore, there is less risk of it being stolen. In addition, asymmetric credentials can provide loosely coupled trust by using certificates, which enables delegation of identity management.

Once authenticated, many systems switch to using a symmetric credential for performance improvements. These credentials have shorter validity period and are not valid outside of the current session, therefore credential exposure is less of a risk. In addition, using separate credentials for each session ensures that a compromise of one session credential does not lead to a compromise of other sessions.

At a high level, most of these systems work like this:

1. The client connects to the service
2. The server provides its certificate containing its public key, along with a list of supported symmetric algorithms
3. The client authenticates the server and ensures it is trusted
4. The client generates a new symmetric credential using one of the mutually supported algorithms

5. The new symmetric credential is encrypted with the server's public key for safe transport to the server

6. Both systems switch to using the symmetric credential

In some cases, the client may send its public key for authentication to the server. This concept is called mutual authentication and ensures the identity of both sides of the communication instead of only authenticating the server.

Examples of this combination are everywhere and include:

- Secure sockets layer (SSL) and transport layer security (TLS)
- The oAuth protocol
- VPN technology using certificate authentication
- Smart card authentication in Kerberos (the PKINIT protocol)

Going the other direction, symmetric authentication can be used to identify a human and unlock use of an asymmetric credential for subsequent use. This technique allows the human to use a simple form of authentication to the device, while still providing asymmetric authentication for any subsequent sessions they establish. One good example of this is Microsoft's Windows Hello authentication.

Public Key Infrastructure

The most common use of asymmetric credentials is with digital certificates. When used in a PKI, the keys in an asymmetric credential pair are classified as a public key and a private key. Public keys are written to digital certificates along with a bunch of optional attributes that describe the principal, approved uses for the key, and details about its validity and issuer.

Certificates

Certificates are the center of a PKI. Certificates work together with cryptography to provide loosely coupled authentication based on asymmetric credentials and digital signatures. These certificates chain together in a parent–child relationship in which trusting a parent certificate implies trust in any certificates digitally signed by its private key.

A certificate is a set of attributes paired together with a public key. Attributes on the certificate include information about the identity of the certificate holder, its validity period, and its intended purpose.

As long as the private key associated with the certificate remains confidential, we can trust that:

- Data encrypted using the private key came from the principal as long as we can decrypt it using the associated public key
- Data encrypted using the public key can only be decrypted by its corresponding private key

Certificate Chaining

Most certificates attributes are digitally signed to enable clients to determine its issuer. The process of determining certificate issuers happens recursively until ultimately either a trusted issuer is identified or a self-signed certificate is reached (one that is not signed by an issuer).

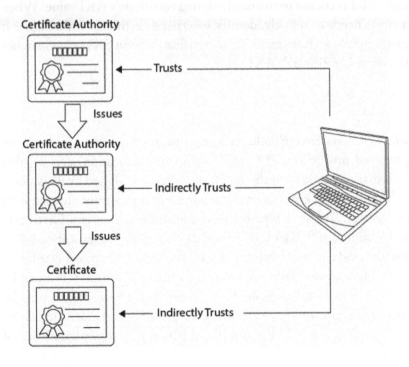

When a certificate is issued, the issuing certificate digitally signs the attributes on the certificate using its private key. The signature and details about the issuing certificate are written to the certificate to enable clients to validate the certificate's issuer using a process called certificate chaining.

A number of new attributes are written to a certificate during the signing process. The first is the issuer, which is a copy of the subject from the signing certificate. This field enables us to determine who issued the certificate in a human readable form.

The second is information on where a client can find the issuer's certificate publicly to enable chain validation. This field, called the Authority Information Access (AIA), should be accessible to any client wishing to validate certificates signed by the certificate and should not change throughout the lifetime of the signing certificate.

To improve chaining performance, certificates use unique identifiers based on a hash of the certificate's public key. These attributes, called the Subject Key Identifier (SKI) and the Authority Key Identifier (AKI), simplify certificate location and improves performance when searching for a certificate's issuer. During signing, the signing certificate's SKI is copied to the newly signed certificate's AKI value. When a client needs to quickly identify whether a certificate is the signer it can simply search its cache for a certificate whose SKI value matches the signed certificate's AKI value.

Revocation

Most PKI systems include revocation to limit the impact of a compromised private key. If the issuer provides revocation services, this information is added to the certificate when it is signed by its issuer.

There are two kinds of revocation information commonly used with certificates. The first type of revocation information is a Certificate Revocation List (CRL). CRLs are the original type of revocation information used and will likely remain in use for backwards compatibility.

A CRL is essentially a list of certificate serial numbers revoked by the CA issued on a periodic basis. These lists are digitally signed by the issuer's private key to guarantee authenticity and placed in a location which is accessible by any client that may need to validate one of its issued certificates. This location is written to the certificate as its CRL Distribution Point, or CDP, during signing.

Over time, the technology industry discovered a major scalability problem with CRLs. CRLs would become very large files as the list of revoked certificates grew, which can severely impact certificate validation performance, increase WAN utilization, and just generally slow everything down. Also, we needed a way to "pause" the validity of certificates – something which the CRL approach wasn't designed to accommodate. As a result, Online Certificate Status Protocol (OCSP) was invented.

OCSP is a lightweight webservice designed to provide high-speed revocation information without the overhead associated with downloading giant CRLs and then validating their signature. An OCSP responder is delegated the ability to provide revocation information when it is given an OCSP signing certificate signed by the issuer.

When a client wants to validate certificate revocation over OCSP, it connects to the responder via SSL and submits the certificate's serial number. The OCSP responder looks up the serial number in its database and provides a response that the certificate is good, revoked, or unknown. This response is digitally signed using its OCSP signing certificate, enabling the client to validate its delegation to provide revocation information on behalf of the issuer.

If an OCSP responder is in use, the URL of the responder will be written to the certificate's AIA attribute during signing.

Constraining Use

Certificates are used for a wide variety of purposes including SSL encryption, authentication of an OCSP responder, identifying a user, and even issuing other certificates. We need to ensure that certificates I issued by that CA are used as intended to protect the integrity of the certificate chain. To accomplish this, certificate issuers typically impose limitations on their issued certificates during the signing process.

A certificate's intended usage is defined by the Key Usage and Extended Key Usage fields. If populated, it is the client's responsibility to ensure that the certificate is being used appropriately during validation.

Certificate Authorities

Most certificate relationships use a server called a certificate authority, or CA. Certificate authorities are servers that manage the cryptographic operations involved in a PKI. They establish a process for certificate signing, maintain a catalog of issued and revoked certificates, automatically publish revocation information, and ensure consistency in attributes assigned to issued certificates.

While important in a PKI, CAs are really only workflow engines which manage certificate operations. A CA can be offline for an extended period of time without consequence as long as its certificate and revocation lists remain valid.

Authentication Protocols

Authentication protocols define the process that principals use to identify themselves to systems. During authentication, sensitive credentials are transmitted between systems. The protocol used during authentication determines the protection of the credential against monitoring attacks or systems masquerading as trusted systems.

Basic Authentication

The simplest authentication protocol is basic authentication. In basic authentication, the credential is transmitted in the clear, thus providing no protection against theft or reuse. Many systems use basic authentication due to its simplicity or to enable humans to authenticate by entering their password into a website.

Basic authentication is used everywhere in the physical world. Any time you present your ID card, use a key to open a lock, identify yourself to your bank over a phone connection, or use biometrics to identify yourself to a computer you are essentially using a form of basic authentication. Most human authentication is basic simply because we aren't usually able to perform advanced math in our heads.

Trustworthy encryption must be implemented beneath the authentication protocol whenever basic authentication is in use. Without it, credential theft is trivial for anyone who can gain access to the network where the authentication occurs. Some examples of this attack include:

- Using a camera to take a picture of a physical ID card, then replicating it
- Listening in on a conversation where a password is spoken
- Sniffing network traffic at a coffee shop and wait for someone to authenticate to a network resource without encryption

In addition, it is important to always authenticate the remote system before performing basic authentication. Without authentication, an attacker may be able to masquerade as a trusted system and trick the system into providing credentials to authenticate the user. For example, an attacker could:

- Install a fake or compromised fingerprint reader to send fingerprints to an attacker-controlled system.
- Use a fake lock to gain an imprint of a key, then replicate it.
- Dress up as a representative of a trusted organization and ask for identification.
- Use a fake hotspot to trick people into thinking they are connecting to their bank website, when it is actually being relayed through their computer.

Hash or Digest Protocols

Hash or digest authentication protocols are only slightly more secure than basic authentication. In a hash authentication protocol, a cryptographic hash of the credential is sent to the remote server instead of the credential itself. The remote system then performs the same operation on its end and compares the two values.

While hash authentication protocols prevent the raw reusable credential from exposure, the attacker can usually determine the credential fairly easily – especially with passwords. Most passwords are predictable; thus, an attacker can use either brute force (continually trying different values until one matches) or a rainbow table (a pre-computed list of hashes for common credentials) to quickly determine the plaintext password.

Another concern is that the hashed credential can be reused multiple times to authenticate to the system. This attack, called a credential replay attack, enables the attacker to masquerade as the compromised identity until the credential is changed.

Challenge Response Protocols

Challenge response protocols are where we start to see security in authentication. Challenge response protocols create one-time credentials by using a unique random value that differs between each authentication attempt. This technique prevents pre-calculated rainbow tables and defends against replay attacks (where an attacker simply captures and retransmits the same response).

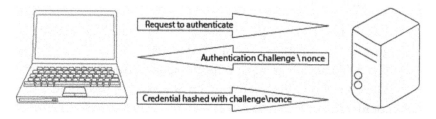

In challenge response authentication, the server generates a random value called a challenge or nonce which uniquely identifies the current authentication session. The challenge is sent to the client, who combines the challenge with the credential and hashes the entire value. The hashed value is sent back to the server, which performs the same operation locally and compares the result.

More secure versions of challenge response protocols may include other session-specific information, such as the time that the response was generated, in the calculation to further complicate analysis.

Federated Authentication Protocols

Federated authentication protocols further improve security and enable single sign-on by authenticating users to services using tokens instead of credentials. This model limits where reusable credentials are stored, transmitted, and exposed thus improving credential confidentiality.

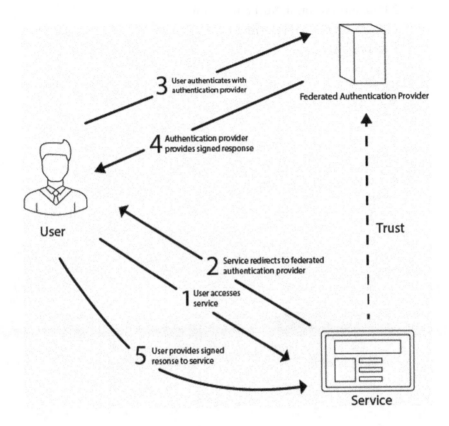

In a federated authentication protocol, requests for authorization-controlled resources are redirected to an authentication server. The authentication server then identifies the client using one or more of the previous authentication protocols. If authentication is successful, a response is generated and signed using the authentication server's credential. This response is sent to the client, which returns to the original resource. The response is then provided to the secured resource as the client's credential which validates the signature on the client's response. If the signature passes, the identity is trusted, and authentication is complete.

Federated authentication protocols are used everywhere, both in enterprise IT and Internet-based authentication systems. Some examples of federated authentication include:

- Microsoft Account Authentication
- Google Identity Platform
- Facebook Logon
- oAuth
- SAML
- OpenID

5

WEAKNESS, VULNERABILITY, AND EXPLOITATION

Weaknesses are flaws or limitations which an attacker can take advantage of to impact the security of a system. These flaws or limitations can enable an attacker to gain illegitimate access to sensitive information, bypass security checks, prevent legitimate use, or cause a wide variety of other security issues. The goal of mitigation should be to limit weak points to an acceptable level for safe operation of the service, not to try and eliminate it altogether.

Weakness Versus Vulnerability

The terms weakness and vulnerability are used interchangeably in information security, but each have a slightly different definition. A weakness is any security condition which may enable compromise. In comparison, a vulnerability is a specific instance of a weakness found within software or within a system.

Weakness

Weaknesses are tracked by Mitre in an online database called the Common Weakness Enumeration, or CWE (https://cwe.mitre.org). Each weakness is a security design flaw or limitation, which may enable an attacker to gain unintended control over a system. Each weakness is assigned an ID and associated with vulnerabilities which are caused in whole or in part by the weakness.

The CWE database is free to use and provides good descriptions and examples of common weaknesses in both software and systems. Some examples of weaknesses include:

Table 5.1

CWE ID	NAME	DESCRIPTION
CWE-20	Improper Input Validation	The product does not validate or incorrectly validates input that can affect the control flow or data flow of a program.
CWE-125	Out-of-bounds Read	The software reads data past the end, or before the beginning, of the intended buffer.
CWE-287	Improper Authentication	When an actor claims to have a given identity, the software does not prove or insufficiently proves that the claim is correct.
CWE-798	Use of Hard-coded Credentials	The software contains hard-coded credentials, such as a password or cryptographic key, which it uses for its own inbound authentication, outbound communication to external components, or encryption of internal data.

Vulnerability

A vulnerability describes a specific instance of a weakness within a software package or system. A vulnerability may be the result of one or more weaknesses and can be tracked to specific versions of software or system configurations which contain the weaknesses.

Mitre tracks many commercial vulnerabilities in a database called Common Vulnerabilities and Exposures, or CVE (https://cve.mitre.org/). Just like weaknesses, each vulnerability is assigned an ID and tracked along with any notifications or patches issued by the software vendor, links to work-arounds, associated weaknesses, and related public posts discussing the topic. Some examples of CVE entries include:

Table 5.2

CVE ID	DESCRIPTION
CVE-2017–11780	The Server Message Block 1.0 (SMBv1) on Microsoft Windows Server 2008 SP2 and R2 SP1, Windows 7 SP1, Windows 8.1, Windows Server 2012 Gold and R2, Windows RT 8.1, Windows 10 Gold, 1511, 1607, and 1703, and Windows Server 2016, allows a remote code execution vulnerability when it fails to properly handle certain requests, aka "Windows SMB Remote Code Execution Vulnerability".
CVE-2019–1326	A denial of service vulnerability exists in Remote Desktop Protocol (RDP) when an attacker connects to the target system using RDP and sends specially crafted requests, aka 'Windows Remote Desktop Protocol (RDP) Denial of Service Vulnerability'.
CVE-2013–5122	Cisco Linksys Routers EA2700, EA3500, E4200, EA4500: A bug can cause an unsafe TCP port to open which leads to unauthenticated access.
CVE-2014–0048	An issue was found in Docker before 1.6.0. Some programs and scripts in Docker are downloaded via HTTP and then executed or used in unsafe ways.

Common Vulnerability Scoring System (CVSS)

Each CVE entry typically includes a measurement of the severity of the vulnerability using the CVSS. The CVSS measures the risk and potential impact a vulnerability can have on a system based on the severity of the vulnerability to the system's security, the maturity of known exploit code for the vulnerability, and the impact that successful exploitation would have on the organization's overall security. The result is a score from 0 to 10 with a higher score indicating a more severe vulnerability.

Semantics

Some professional organizations use these terms interchangeably, such as the Open Web Application Security Project, or OWASP (https:// owasp.org). The terms are synonyms of each other, and most information security professionals collectively refer to both as vulnerability.

This book commonly interchanges the terms weakness and vulnerability. We are doing this because we are talking about weaknesses within your organization which would then be tracked internally as a vulnerability. In addition, the ability to interchange the terms makes the book more readable. Where possible, I will use the most correct term for the scenario.

Understanding Vulnerability

Vulnerabilities consist of three major parts: the vulnerability type, the associated weakness or weaknesses, and the state at which the system or its data are vulnerable. Each part determines part of the plan for mitigating or remediating the vulnerability.

Types of Vulnerability

The type of a vulnerability identifies the party who can fully remediate the risk. While mitigating factors can reduce the exposure of a risk, it cannot be fully eliminated without eliminating the risks' source, which at some point means making the capability unavailable.

Vulnerabilities occur as one of three general types: logic vulnerabilities, implementation vulnerabilities, or limitation vulnerabilities

Logic Vulnerabilities   A logic vulnerability is something within the instructions of how the service carries out its capability. Most of the vulnerabilities tracked in the National Vulnerability Database are software logic vulnerabilities – errors made in design which cause the service or component to become untrustworthy in some capacity. Some examples of software weaknesses which lead to logic vulnerabilities include:

- Memory corruption
- Command injection
- Improper pointer handling
- Cross-site scripting (XSS)
- Lack of input validation

Logic vulnerabilities aren't limited to software. Flaws in decision making, physical security products, or process design are also logic vulnerabilities. For example, in social engineering, an attacker deceives their target or leverages cognitive biases to cause them to perform unauthorized activity. These "bugs" coded into our psyche pose a risk when individuals are entrusted with making security decisions.

A logic vulnerability in hardware is an unpredicted weakness to attack in the physical design of the device. This might be use of too weak of a metal on a safe, the ability to use a magnet to bypass a locking mechanism, or a predictable or deducible code on a padlock.

Implementation Vulnerabilities   Imagine you are reviewing the security of a building. In your review, you find that there is a tree immediately adjacent to the fence intended to prevent unauthorized entry. The fence would be effective if it weren't for the tree; therefore, it's a flaw in how the system was designed rather than a flaw in the fence itself.

Implementation vulnerabilities are the result of improper design. This class of vulnerability is the responsibility of the architect that designed the system rather than the creator of its components.

Sometimes system implementation vulnerabilities are created as shortcuts to simplify management. For example, granting a security principal extra authorization or granting unnecessary authorization to principals through membership may be easier than explicitly identifying each principal's individual needs. This may become an issue if too many shortcuts are taken since the cumulative result may expose the system to unnecessary risk.

Software implementation vulnerabilities typically stem from either misconfiguration of an otherwise secure component, overly integrated components, overprivileged principles, or exposure of credentials. Some weaknesses which lead to implementation vulnerabilities include:

- Lack of encryption of sensitive data
- Exposure of reusable credentials to high risk systems
- Granting unnecessary privileges to a securable which enable it to compromise system security
- Reusing the same credentials for different principles

In the physical world, implementation vulnerabilities are systemic weaknesses in an otherwise sound design. In other words, the individual components within the system are presumed reliable but their assembly places the system at risk. Some examples of implementation vulnerabilities in the physical world include:

- A high-security building which has windows installed on the first floor
- Use of a weak lock or chain to secure an otherwise strong fence
- Improper installation of a security product, such as having barbed wire facing the wrong direction or placing a security fence directly adjacent to a tree
- Use of a strong key code lock with a weak code
- Not encrypting sensitive information at the file level, thus losing the ability to control it if stolen

In process design, implementation vulnerabilities are typically found where trust is inherent, or authentication is weak or missing. These conditions can turn an otherwise secure human process into vulnerability simply by accepting untrusted input. Examples include:

- An acquisition process that doesn't validate that the purchased product came from a trusted supplier.
- A facility security process which accepts ID cards from an unverifiable source as authentication, such as the "any card or

letter with your name on it" approach used by some government offices.

- An inconsistent authentication process for access to the same facility, such as a "VIP" entrance where authentication is optional to an otherwise secure facility.
- A process which has an emergency workaround which can be invoked by an external untrusted source (e.g., a process where an unvalidated person states that there is a fire which causes the guard to unsecure doors out of concern for safety).
- Outsourcing the ability to grant administrative authorization on behalf of the customer organization.

Limitation   Limitation vulnerabilities occur when a component of a system has a capacity which can be exceeded or overcome. The result of overcoming the limitation depends on the type of control and the way the limitation is being exceeded.

The physical world is full of limitations, partially because we live in a multidimensional space. Physical world components are naturally limited by their strength, dimensions, capacity, and composition among other factors. Exceeding these limitations can result in illegitimate access being granted or legitimate access being denied. Some examples of physical world limitation vulnerabilities include:

- Climbing or flying over a wall or fence
- Using a weapon to break through a door, wall, or other barrier
- Cutting a padlock's shackle
- A protest blocking an entrance to a building
- Cutting off an enemy's access to supplies

In the virtual world, limitations are somewhat more bound due to their existence in a somewhat "flat" space. Many limitation vulnerabilities in the cyber space are derived from either an inability to service a legitimate request due to a large volume of data or cryptographic or other key-based mathematical limitations. For example:

- Legitimate access to a service being denied by flooding the system with noise, such as in a distributed denial of service attack.
- Limitations in an algorithm's key space which enable an attacker to guess or derive a legitimate key during its validity (such as brute force guessing a password).

- Stealing sensitive information from system memory while it is unencrypted for use.
- Monitoring electromagnetic emanations to reproduce data being processed by the system (e.g., a sideband or TEMPEST attack).

Human examples of limitation vulnerabilities differ in that they focus on human susceptibilities – a condition which every person has but differs in effect based on their beliefs and personal situation. For example:

- A person can be bribed, especially if they have financial troubles.
- A person's inner beliefs can be used to coerce otherwise protected information.
- Blackmail can be used to force them to disclose confidential information or perform activities they otherwise wouldn't.

The human limit concept obviously extends beyond these options, though I believe these examples provide enough context.

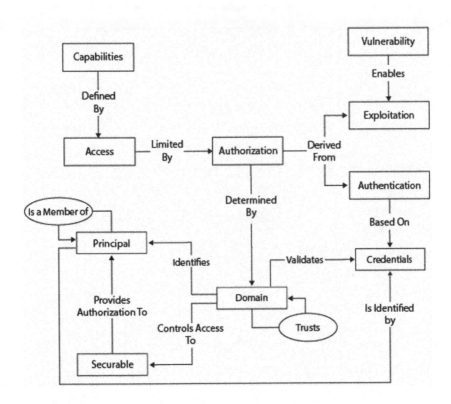

6

IMPACT

While it is convenient to focus on the vulnerable component in an attack, this is rarely the target of interest. In most cases, successful exploitation of a vulnerability leads to multiple potential forms of impact which provide significantly greater value than the target itself. Think about a thief – the reason they bypass the lock on a car door isn't that they are interested in the lock or the door, but rather the valuables secured within the car, or to steal the car itself.

Imagine you pick the lock on a security fence surrounding an otherwise protected building. At a macro level you could say your ability to exploit a weak authentication system resulted in your new ability to access the area surrounded by fence, but the true impact is your ability to now access the unlocked window or door which relied on the integrity of the fence as its security boundary. Many security designs rely on the integrity of other security controls as part of their protection strategy. In this case, the unlocked window or door relied on the integrity of the security fence and lock – and in bypassing those protections you can gain control over resources.

In technology, this is akin to trusting a firewall or other boundary to protect an otherwise vulnerable system. These protections are usually trustworthy until either a vulnerable device exposed to the edge is exploited or a compromised machine is brought within the protected zone. In either of these cases, once inaccessible services become accessible to the attacker, thus providing avenues to further compromise.

Vulnerabilities and Impact

Both vulnerabilities and impact reduce the security of an organization, but there is one key differentiator. A vulnerability in a system exists in the system's natural state. In other words, the attacker didn't need to do anything to make the vulnerability appear – it was already there. Impact, on the other hand, is a change to the security of a system based on an attacker's action. In many cases, impact creates a net-new vulnerability within the system.

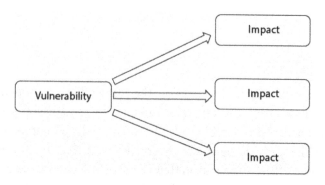

A single vulnerability typically provides a variety of potential forms of impact, each of which providing different value to the attacker. The choice made by the attacker is typically defined by their motive and may only represent one step in a larger attack campaign.

Vulnerability and Impact Example: Webshell

Imagine the victim is a vulnerable webserver with a remote code execution vulnerability. If successful, the attacker gains the ability to run arbitrary commands on the underlying server using the identity of the website.

Let's say the attacker decides to use this vulnerability to compromise the integrity of the website by writing a webshell to a web published directory. At this point, the attacker has chosen a form of impact to use with the vulnerability by compromising the integrity of the website. The creation of the webshell is the impact aspect of the attack.

The webshell provides the attacker durable access and authorization within the environment. The attacker will maintain this control even if the administrator or developer finds and fixes the vulnerable code – as long as they don't find the webshell.

Most attacks don't stop there. The attacker can now access a bunch of resources that were previously secured. As a result, once secure components now become vulnerable and the cycle repeats again.

We'll return to this scenario later in the chapter to analyze the impact of this persistence.

Persistence

In most breaches, success requires an attacker to exploit multiple vulnerabilities, each getting the attacker one step closer to their target. Attackers must maintain durable access and authorization to compromised components to accomplish this. This means the attacker must make a change to the compromised component after exploitation at each major milestone throughout the compromise.

Persistence is a form of access, authorization, or authentication created within the system by an attacker, which provides them illegitimate durable control. Successful persistence can enable an attacker to access resources which would otherwise be protected.

Durability is the key value of persistence. Technically an attacker could exploit the same vulnerability repeatedly, each time adding additional steps to get them closer to their goal. The problem is that this behavior is noisy, unreliable, and likely to be detected over time. If the vulnerability is detected and fixed, the attacker would lose access or authorization, thus forcing them to search for a new vulnerability to exploit.

Persistence ultimately traces back to a loss of integrity within the system. Integrity is derived from the ability to trust the state of the system and its components; therefore, an attacker must obtain write authorization to persist – through either authentication or exploitation. This means the attacker must create or change something providing them illegitimate control, such as:

- Installing a piece of illegitimate remote access software or malware on a compromised host
- Tampering with or destroying an access control to provide illegitimate access to assumed protected services
- Creation of a fake ID card or use of a stolen reusable credential to provide illegitimate authentication
- Getting a spy hired in a key role within the target organization
- Modifying an authentication system to enable acceptance of illegitimate credentials

The Impact of Persistence

After persistence, the attacker will likely gain the ability to access services available to their newly compromised component. This means that any systems or components which once relied on access boundaries for protection now solely rely on authorization controls for protection.

Persistence may also provide the attacker authorization up to the level of the compromised component. In other words, the attacker may gain the ability to perform anything which the compromised component can perform within the system. This may include the ability to authenticate to remote services if the component runs under an identity trusted by other components or systems.

A third possibility with persistence is the ability to attack other users of the system by proxy. This could enable the attacker to reflect an attack to other users of the system, thus turning a once trusted system into an attack vector.

Authorization Persistence

Persistence can be established through authorization by modifying an authorization control mechanism, such as an access control list. For example, a change to an access control list that grants additional principals authorization to the system can be used to provide a backdoor into the affected component or system.

Let's say you were a spy who gained legitimate access to your victim facility. If possible, you might consider adding additional illegitimate individuals to an access list or modify software configurations to allow malicious use of their services. In these cases, the actual impact was simply a reconfiguration of an otherwise secure system.

Imagine your target lives in a gated community with a guard and an access list. To gain persistent entry into the community, you could try to trick the guard into thinking you are your target and ask them to add someone to their access list. The initial exploit (socially engineering the guard) provided the ability to write to the access list, which you then used to modify the list of individuals allowed to enter.

Authentication Persistence

Persistence through authentication occurs when an attacker gains the ability to create a backdoor account or modify an existing principal to add an additional credential. This might mean setting the password for an existing (but perhaps stale) user account, adding an additional form of authentication which resolves to that identity, or modifying the authentication system to provide a "skeleton key" which can be used to authenticate as any principal.

Going back to our gated community example, what if you added a new vehicle to someone's list of cars instead of tricking the guard to add you to the list of approved guests. This might result in them creating a new vehicle sticker. In this case, you've added a credential to a preexisting identity and gained the ability to authenticate as them.

True authentication persistence means that the identity must legitimately be valid for the system. For example, creating a high-quality fake ID card is technically exploiting a vulnerability and not a form of persistence. True authentication persistence results from a change in the integrity of authentication within the system. In other words, the attacker must be able to write to or create an identity which is legitimately accepted by the system for authentication.

Note that credential theft is not a form of authentication persistence since full control of the credential is not in the attacker's hands. This is because the legitimate owner of the principal can change their credential or invalidate the existing one, thus removing the attacker's ability to authenticate. Real authentication persistence means that an administrative action must be taken to remove the attacker's ability to authenticate to the system. While credential theft provides some durability, it is ultimately outside of the attacker's control.

Access Persistence

Persistence can also be accomplished by modifying an access control. In this type of persistence, the attacker obtains the ability to change or modify how the access control works to allow illegitimate use of an otherwise secured system.

Access persistence in the physical world typically means destroying or eliminating some form of barrier. This could be removal of a grate, destruction of a wall, or modification of a barrier designed to prevent passage. In our previous example, it would become access persistence had the spy removed the door instead of simply leaving it unlocked.

From a technology perspective, access persistence could be accomplished through changing a firewall configuration to enable otherwise blocked network addresses to communicate with a sensitive service.

Like our other examples, it is important to differentiate persistence from vulnerability. While establishing access persistence creates a new vulnerability, it was not in the original design. All persistence involves an attacker causing a change to access, authorization, or authentication which bypasses the intended capability.

Tamper

Another form of integrity impact is tamper, whereby the attacker modifies a system or its data. Tamper is similar to persistence, though it is performed without the intent to establish and maintain durable control over the component. Instead, tamper attacks change how the system operates or its results.

One of the best examples of a tamper attack occurred when Stuxnet malware infected nuclear refinement systems in Iran. Once infected, it caused a slight change to the way centrifuges operated resulting in damaged centrifuges and, more importantly, ruined uranium samples.

Supply Chain Attacks

A supply chin attack focuses on partners involved in its target's business relationships or supply network. Depending on the attack, this might involve tampering with physical distribution of products used by the target, a vendor software update process, or communications with trusted business partners.

One recent example of a supply chain attack occurred when an attacker compromised Solarwinds software update processes, thereby allowing the attackers to push a backdoor into any customer running their Orion software. This attack potentially compromised 18,000 customers including government agencies, security firms, technology firms, and more. This attack went undetected for at least eight months.

Another reason to leverage a supply chain attack is to gain control over multiple victims from a single compromise. For example, the cyberattack group "Barium" has been known to add backdoors to software vendor source code which then gets published as an update by the vendor. As a result, the attacker's malware is installed on the machines of any users who install the malicious update.

Fraud

Fraud is defined as intentional deception to secure unfair or unlawful gain, or to deprive a victim of a legal right. These attacks leverage forged information to coerce a target into performing an action which causes harm.

Perhaps the most common examples of fraud pertain to illicit money transfer. For example, an attacker may compromise the email of a person in corporate finance and use their email address to instruct a bank to perform a wire transfer.

Reflective Attacks

A reflective attack uses an attacker's ability to write to compromise the system's users. These attacks leverage the trusted aspect of the system as a delivery vehicle for malware, propaganda, or other malicious content.

A common example of a reflective attack in technology is a watering hole attack. Attackers leveraging this technique will compromise a website they expect their targets to visit and use it as a delivery mechanism for malware. Unknowing users connect to the site and usually inherently trust its content, thereby simplifying delivery of malware.

One example of a watering hole attack occurred in 2013 when an attacker compromised the veteran's affairs website and used it to exploit a previously unknown vulnerability in Internet Explorer and

Java. This attack targeted active duty military and veterans of the US Department of Defense, many of which likely held positions at sensitive government organizations.

A human variant of a reflective attack typically occurs on social media. These attacks use fake identities to influence audiences through specially crafted propaganda. Although many publicly regard social media as an untrustworthy medium, these ideas spread by being reshared through networks of trusted individuals, ultimately laundering its origination. In this way, a medium which is regarded as untrustworthy becomes a trusted source when people they trust reshare or repost the propaganda. For a great example of how this works, check out the book Information Wars by Richard Stengel.

Theft and Espionage

An espionage attack leverages an attacker's ability to read and transmit sensitive information from their target. This form requires the attacker to gain read access to their target's otherwise protected information. As with any form of impact, the data stolen by the attacker must have been protected had they not gained the ability to read it illegitimately.

Theft or espionage is essentially an attacker taking physical property, sensitive information, intellectual property, or really anything to which they have both access and authorization.

Credential Theft

We have all seen a movie where the spy secretly steals a badge from an employee of an organization and uses it to get through doors. This is an example of credential theft – a condition where an attacker gains read access to a credential and either steals or replicates it. If successful, the attacker can use it anywhere it is accepted for as long as it remains valid.

Credential theft should not be confused with credential persistence. In credential theft, there is presumably a legitimate principal actively using the credential. This means that the attacker cannot change the credential without disrupting the legitimate activity and ultimately "tipping their hand". That said, the attacker may be able to use the stolen credential to persist if enables the attacker to create a new principal or tamper with the integrity of the system.

In the software world, credential theft is commonly performed by stealing passwords, password derivatives, or session credentials. Passwords are easiest as many are created by humans and follow predictable patterns. Even difficult ones are typed onto keyboards causing them to be susceptible to visual monitoring and keystroke logging.

Stealing credential derivatives or session credentials typically requires the attacker to read either system memory or network communication. Once stolen, these credentials may be able to be injected to create new illegitimate sessions masquerading as the original principal, thereby granting the attacker any authorization granted to the principal to any service which accepts it.

The most pervasive credential theft attack in recent history has been pass the hash, whereby the attacker steals a session credential from system memory and uses it to create new illegitimate sessions for up to as long as the credential is valid. This technique can be detrimental to organizations where a single identity source is used for authentication to a large number of systems, or where a single credential is shared across multiple computers.

Destruction

Destructive impact occurs when an attacker destroys the availability or utility of a system or its data. These attacks range in scope from disabling a specific service to elimination of an entire system or its data altogether. Destructive attacks in the physical world are fairly straightforward, so we will be focusing on how a destructive attack works in the cyber realm.

Wiper

A wiper attack makes data unavailable for legitimate use. In a wiper attack, the data are destroyed with the intention of making it unrecoverable. These attacks typically go through each file on a system and delete them. In most cases, the file's data are overwritten with random data to ensure that the data are removed from the file system.

Cryptographic Ransom

In cryptographic ransom, the attacker uses encryption to affect the file's utility. In other words, the file may be wholly intact, but unreadable without the attacker's key. These attacks are usually financially motivated and demand payment using some form of cryptocurrency.

Vulnerability Chaining

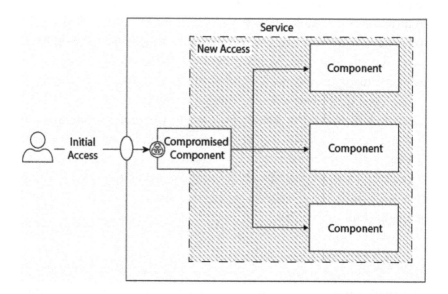

Most attacks involve multiple cycles of vulnerability identification, exploitation, and impact. Each time an attacker identifies and successfully exploits a weakness in a system, they gain additional capability in hopes that it will get them closer to their goal. This process is referred to as vulnerability chaining.

There are two main classes of vulnerabilities which enable an attacker to pivot and gain additional control over their target: system integrity vulnerabilities and credential confidentiality vulnerabilities. While all impact is detrimental to the target's security, these two classes lead to an attacker either establishing persistence within the system or attaining additional authorization.

Back to Our Webshell Example

Earlier in the chapter, we discussed a scenario whereby an attacker exploits a vulnerable website and uses it to copy a webshell to a web-published directory. Let's return to that example and see what the attacker might be able to do now that they've persisted on the webserver.

Access   The first aspect of this compromise to consider becomes where the webserver can route connections. Typically, the webserver will be able to access services which were unavailable to the public due to a firewall or other network restriction. These services may enable the attacker to control otherwise secured aspects of the system, such as access to:

- Internal name resolution
- Databases which support the webserver's operation
- Internal authentication systems
- Remote administration capabilities, such as SSH, RDP, or remote PowerShell

Authorization   The second aspect of the compromise pertains to the identity of the website and its authorization. Many websites are part of a larger system which may include back-end services or databases which the attacker may gain access to. This could mean the ability to run arbitrary queries on the database, steal or modify information on back-end systems, or the ability to authenticate as the web application to dependent services outside the system.

If the identity of the webserver is trusted by other components in the system, such as when a single sign-on solution is used, the attacker may be able to establish new authenticated sessions using this identity to services not intended for use by the webserver. For example, the identity may have been granted excessive authorization resulting in the website having administrative permissions to other servers.

The third aspect is the integrity of the content provided by the website. If the attacker has the ability to modify the application (such as changing a web page) they may be able to use it to deliver illegitimate content to unsuspecting users. For example, the attacker might use the website to deliver malware to its users or steal their login credentials.

Authentication   If the compromised website uses a principal with administrative authorization, the attacker may be able to compromise other sessions on the webserver or expose credentials of other applications or users of the server. These credentials can enable the attacker to masquerade as the compromised principals and leverage their authorization.

PART 2
DESIGNING AND OPERATING A SECURE SYSTEM

7
IDENTIFY

Creation of a secure system begins by identifying what it is you want to secure. While this sounds easy, putting a quantitative value on the security of information can be a challenge. The natural desire is to say that everything is important, but with limited resources available for security we must be diligent about identifying exactly how valuable everything is – and from what perspective.

Identifying and classifying the types of information, capabilities, and credentials within a system is more of an art than a science today. We do our best to measure the impact of loss of these assets, but this is usually an educated guess.

What to Classify

There are three main aspects of a system to consider when designing a classification system. Each will require a different approach, and in many cases, a different classification scheme.

Data

Our first thing to classify is data. Data are the static information used or provided by the system. It includes files, documents, plans, research results, specifications, and other information used by the system and its users as part of the system's operation.

Services

The second aspect of a system to classify is any services it provides. Services are essentially the kinetic capabilities of the system which provide capabilities. These capabilities define what the system is used for – its purpose. These services might be directly consumed by users, or be subsumed as infrastructure for other services like authentication, name resolution, or routing.

Principals

Third, we need to classify principals. Going back to our authorization concepts, principals are identities to which authorization can be granted. At a basic level, this authorization is either user or administrative depending on whether it can be used to circumvent the security of the system itself.

The value of a principal is derived from the sum of all its authorizations. Classification occurs at the principal level to simplify tracking because tracking and classifying every credential derived from an authenticated principal is nearly impossible, especially when dealing with ephemeral session credentials.

On the other extreme, classifying based on authorization doesn't represent operational risk accurately. While we know that administrative permissions to key services poses risk, we can't quantify how many principals have that authorization or their credential exposure by classifying the authorization. Identifying principals with the authorization gives us an idea of the amount of potential exposure inherent to the system.

How to Classify

Most classification schemas leverage a label-based system. These systems identify assets based on their potential impact to the organization, either directly or indirectly.

A classification system needs to be understandable to be effective. Classifying the value of each individual piece of data or capability is just as bad as not having a classification system at all. In the end, its best to organize and value concepts into three or four categories of sensitivity or value. It is best to keep the basics simple and leave the detailed implementation aspects to your information security professionals.

Confidentiality Sensitivity

Confidentiality-sensitive assets are the first types of sensitive documents that come to mind when we think about data classification. Confidentiality sensitive documents and services commonly represent either an advantage for one organization over another, strategic plans, or sensitive financial or customer information.

The biggest issue with confidentiality is that once it is lost it cannot be reclaimed. While you may be able to reestablish control of a document encrypted with digital rights management, any information lost while the attacker had control remains lost. There is no way to truly reestablish confidentiality short of destroying the attacker, any copies or derived information they may have produced, and anyone they may have shared the stolen information with.

Integrity Sensitivity

Integrity-sensitive assets are those where unauthorized changes represent significant risk to the organization. Common examples of integrity sensitive assets include financial records, critical internal operations, authentication stores, and trust configurations.

Once tampered with, integrity can be difficult to restore. In many cases, you may be faced with trading off data loss for improved confidence in the system's integrity. This will also need to be balanced with the availability of backups or integrity check information.

Availability Sensitivity

An availability sensitive asset is one which causes significant business impact when it is offline or unable to scale for demand. These may be business critical processes, physical facilities, high value dependencies, or other key operational components which hinder or halt important systems when unavailable for use.

Unlike other forms of sensitivity, an availability sensitive asset typically does not have effects which stretch beyond the period of nonavailability. That said, restoration of an availability sensitive asset may have the longest recovery time. For example, recovery can be very time-consuming and costly if an attacker destroys a building at a base, a database and its associated backups, or key personnel in an operation.

Measuring Impact

We need some means of quantifying a sensitive asset's impact on the organization to enable them to be ranked and classified. While it may be convenient to focus on the asset itself, it is rarely the most impactful. Many times, the costliest impact of loss of a sensitive asset is its impact to strategy, operations, brand reputation, or other intangibles which can be difficult to measure.

Direct Impact

To start, let's look at the impact of loss of confidentiality of data from a research and development effort. The most obvious impact in this case is in the form of competitive advantage. Most research and development are performed to capture a portion of market value, thus justifying its investment. Research and development efforts can cost millions of dollars in time and materials, a cost avoided if the resulting intellectual property is stolen.

Presumably, the attacker (or the attacker's client) plans to use this intellectual property to enter the market themselves. This reduces the competitive advantage gained from research, thereby reducing the value returned since a competitor may be able to develop a product with equal capabilities at a lower cost.

Other forms of direct impact could involve operational readiness, project delays, regulatory fines, or financial fraud. Each of these conditions has its own quantifiable impact.

Indirect Impact

Other forms of impact are more indirect – affecting the organization through reputation, partnership, or other soft metrics which may be difficult to quantify. This includes a variety of intangible aspects of the system including brand reputation, trust, and perception which stem from outside perception of the breach.

Imagine an attacker finds a vulnerability in a government organization's website and uses it for defacement. Perception of the potential impact of the breach may cause the public to believe that the compromise is more deeply rooted than it actually is – especially if amplified by speculation performed by news coverage. This could cause the reputation of the organization to be damaged beyond what is warranted, and may cause efforts to clarify the real impact to be perceived as a cover-up.

Measuring Loss Expectancy

One common way to measure risk leverages a financial model to determine the estimated cost if the organization were to lose security over an asset. While subjective, this approach is very effective in describing security risk to leadership.

Costs associated with loss are usually expressed in financial terms, but could also be represented in any metric the organization uses for success. For example, some organizations might not have a profit motive, but there is always some "currency" which leadership uses to measure the success of their operation. We will talk about cost in terms of money to keep things simple and applicable to most private sector companies.

To begin, we need to value the amount of money that a compromise of security over an asset would cost. This value, called the single loss expectancy (SLE), should not take into account any security mitigations that are in-place to reduce the likelihood or impact of compromise (we will get to this in the next chapter). Be sure to include any monetary value associated with the loss, including:

- Direct recovery costs
- Lost productivity
- Missed opportunities
- Operational impact

Once you've determined the SLE, estimate the approximate number of times that you would expect this type of compromise to happen in a year. This value, the annualized rate of occurrence (ARO), should be a decimal and can be less than zero if loss is expected to occur less than once per year. For example:

- If you expect the loss to happen once per year, the ARO would be 1.
- If you expect the loss to happen every five years, the ARO would be 0.2.
- If you expect the loss to happen three times per year, the ARO would be 3.

Last, we multiply the SLE and the ARO together to get the annualized loss expectancy (ALE). The ALE enables business leaders to plot the estimated cost on an annual basis and enables them to compare it to other annual investments.

The ALE is a mostly subjective calculation based on statistics and experience. Its best to revisit these numbers periodically to improve their accuracy and update based on new developments.

Inheritance

When classifying assets, be sure to consider their interrelationship with other systems and processes. Always classify assets based on the highest potential classification of any system, data, or principals it is involved with. In other words, if a service provides a capability required by a higher tier service it should be categorized at least at the same level as that higher-tier service.

Sponsorship

Ensure that a sponsor is identified for each system during classification. Sponsors may need to defend justifications and budget expenditure associated with protection of the asset; therefore, they must be leaders within the organization.

Sponsors are also typically involved with determining protective measures associated with a given asset classification. We will dive further into these protections in our next chapter on protection.

Example: US Department of Defense Information Classification

Perhaps the most well-known example of a classification system is used by defense organizations around the world to prevent sensitive documents from reaching enemy hands. Anyone who has seen a few spy movies has seen top secret documents which are either the target of either the hero or the antagonist. Let's look at an example of one of these classification systems, the US Department of Defense (DoD) classification system, to help facilitate our understanding of how a classification system works.

The primary goal of the DoD classification system is to protect national secrets from unauthorized exposure. This means that the "currency" used to describe risk is impact to national security rather than money. Because of this, labels used to identify sensitive data are based on risk to national security. These labels are:

- Confidential: information which could potentially damage national security
- Secret: information which could potentially cause serious damage to national security
- Top secret: information that could potentially cause exceptionally grave damage to national security

Defense classification systems are designed to protect loss of confidentiality because they are focused on unauthorized disclosure. This means that anyone who might encounter a classified asset should know its associated handling procedures and expected protection measures. Using a simple three label system makes this possible.

For those who are very familiar with this system – yes, there are many levels of special categories of the most sensitive documents. Those familiar with these types of classifications are also the same ones who are taught the special handling procedures, and all are still labeled top secret for familiarity. To keep things simple, we are avoiding the intricate nuances associated with the DoD classification system and instead focusing on the general aspects which are applicable to most well-designed programs.

The data classified by this system are identified by original classification authorities, or OCAs. These individuals are effectively sponsors that determine the types of information that should be classified and the sensitivity level associated with it. This ensures that information is freely available by default, and that the organization doesn't waste time and money on unnecessary protective measures for unclassified documents.

We'll dive into some of the protections imparted by this system in our next chapter.

8
PROTECT

In the previous chapter, we performed identification of sensitive information, and the services and principals which possess either legitimate or administrative authorization to them. These are ultimately what we must strive to defend against attack, abuse, or destruction.

Protection is designing the defensive strategy around the assets we've previously identified as being sensitive. In this chapter, we discuss the processes involved with protecting a secure system from abuse by attackers, insider threats, human or technical error, and other threats.

As we go through this chapter, you'll notice the distinct difference in how protection strategies are designed for technology solutions when compared to physical or human process solutions. Many times, physical and human process security is limited by human processing capability. In other words, while encryption and digital signature are a viable strategy for a computer, it is unlikely to be effective outside of the technology realm. This highlights some of the benefits of implementing the core processes of a system in software. That said, the ease at which software allows for data to be shared or stolen means we need to be ever vigilant when designing and analyzing our system's protection strategy.

Identifying Edges

An edge is the boundary of security protection that separates differing systems or security levels. Any form of access traversing an edge represents an opportunity for attack. A single system may have multiple edges depending on the resolution of your analysis. For example:

- The system itself has an edge of services where the trusted internals of the system meet an untrusted external environment, such as the outside world, the Internet, or where the supply chain interacts with public sources or destinations.

- Each component within the system likely has its own edge, which separates the internals of the component from the rest of the system, such as an application, virtual machine, internal department, or segmented off section of a building.
- An additional edge may involve external partners who are involved in the system, such as supply or distribution partners, a single building within a secure facility, or external authentication, analysis, or other software services.

Knowing where the edges of a system are enables you to implement an efficient and effective protection strategy. Each time a service or component traverses an edge, we should define the security requirements for doing so.

From Monolithic Design to Microservices

Many systems can be defined as either a single large system with many components or an integration of multiple smaller systems each having their own edge.

Larger or more complex systems tend to be more difficult to protect due to the increased number of access points. These systems are typically referred to as monolithic systems and suffer from the high degree of complexity and interdependency.

In contrast, systems defined as a long list of smaller components result in simpler test cases and tend to operate more securely and reliably. This is because each component within the system can be tested individually, thus each change is ultimately less impactful to the overall security of the system. In technology, we typically refer to this as microservice design.

Vulnerabilities in a monolithic system tend to have farther reaching implications due to the number of access points available to each component. This means that a security breach in a monolithic system is likely to be more severe and farther-reaching than those occurring in a microservice.

Another challenge that commonly accompanies monolithic systems is the overall breadth of authorization granted to principals. Monolithic systems tend to use fewer security principals with broader authorization when compared to microservices where each component has a defined edge. This occurs because the edge of the system is defined more broadly, thus more individual components are deemed internal, and fewer principals are favored for the purpose of simplicity. This simpler design increases the value of each principal within the system and, when paired with an increased number of points of access, means the impact of credential theft is more detrimental to the security of the system as a whole.

Monolithic systems typically require additional testing when changes are made because more functionality is involved in the defined system boundary. This also means any changes run the risk of broader reliability issues due to the larger number of capabilities exposed at each point of access. In contrast, a microservice has a very small scope of functionality and less complexity which means changes are easier to test and errors are easier to address.

Despite the benefits of microservices, it is important to avoid defining a microservice too tightly. At a certain point, the overhead associated with threat modeling and defining and analyzing security boundaries becomes inefficient. This is where the "art" of security architecture exists – knowing where to set boundaries.

Multi-Session Components

Modern systems commonly have multiple edges, one defined for each type of sensitive data or control processed. For example, modern computers typically support multiple isolated user sessions. These sessions are likely to contain information of different sensitivities, each with its own list of security requirements. In these cases, a system may have multiple edges spread across each session or a single session which has multiple edges because it processes data of multiple sensitivities.

It is important to avoid the rather militant approach of full isolation of information of different sensitivities to protection of only the most sensitive information. The air gap approach is costly and can significantly increase operational overhead if you are not careful. While alternatives to air gap isolation may pose some residual risk, the benefit of utility is likely to outweigh the operational overhead of ensuring total isolation.

The Three Basic Protection Strategies

In general, there are three basic strategies which you can adopt to protect information. Each strategy uses our concepts of access and authorization controls with different benefits and implications. For the purposes of these protections, we are focusing on protecting information confidentiality and integrity. We will discuss protecting availability separately.

Using an Access Control on the Service

At the most basic level, a system can protect sensitive information by implementing an access control. Access controls do not protect the information itself. Rather, they protect information by limiting the ability to get to it. This approach protects the confidentiality and integrity of the information at the cost of utility but does not typically protect the information after it leaves the system.

Using an access control values the security of data over its utility. For example, we might choose to put a firewall in front of the service to prevent exposure of unintended forms of access. This could mean:

- Blocking access to administrative services
- Limiting the source networks from where access can be performed
- Forcing all communications through a network path which can be monitored
- Enforcing principals which access a service to meet a specified baseline compliance

Each of these provides a benefit to the security of the overall system, though some come with a cost. For example, blocking access to administrative services means that an administrator may be unable to respond to an outage from home. Blocking source networks might prevent legitimate collaboration occuring from those network ranges.

The information itself remains unprotected after we surpass the access control. If an attacker were to bypass or destroy the access control, any information protected by that control would be subject to theft, tamper, or destruction.

This also means that the information would be unprotected after it left the system. Imagine a legitimate employee downloads the files to their laptop. The laptop is then stolen by an attacker who can access any unencrypted portions offline. By itself, access controls afford no protection over the information they defend once that information bypasses the edge.

Using an Access Control on the Service Paired With an Authorization Control

Our second approach is to use a technique common in traditional network security design: using an access control paired with an authorization control. This method forces principals to authenticate and be compared to an access control list prior to being provided access. This means we increase the security of the service itself by limiting utility from unauthenticated clients. Using our example, we might:

- Implement a VPN paired with a firewall to force authentication of legitimate principals
- Enforce authentication on the service itself to prevent illegitimate use
- Limit access to devices registered to the organization by requiring a certificate or other form of authentication

This approach increases the utility when compared to solely using an access control but increases potential exposure as a result. Allowing access means we run the risk of attack, through either a credential vulnerability or a software vulnerability. That said, many times the value of increased utility outweighs the additional risk.

We also still have the same risk of the information being exposed outside the service. While we may constrain the initial form of access to the information, we fail to protect the information itself. An attacker can still steal the laptop which had previously downloaded the files.

Using an Authorization Control on the Information

Our third, and most effective, strategy is to protect the information itself with an authorization control. For example, we might consider encrypting the data itself to limit utility to only those with the associated key.

The closer we apply our protection strategy to the information itself, the more effective it becomes. By protecting the information rather than the ability to access it, we can reduce risk of its loss. Using our laptop theft example, the information stolen by the thief would be of no use without the associated key. Because of this, we can be confident in the protection of the information up to our level of confidence in the level of complexity, exposure, and validity periods of credentials which would be able to decrypt the information.

Applying an authorization control directly to the information typically has the highest overhead. Human processes are unlikely to use this strategy without the aid of technology due to the complexity involved with good encryption. Some technology solutions will also favor another strategy in the interest of speed.

The Three States of Information

Information exists in one of three states: in transit, in use, or at rest. When designing our protection strategy, it is important to consider each state separately as threats to each differ significantly.

Protection at-rest strategies control the ability to interact with a static instance of information. These defenses are designed into the system to ensure secure operation. For example:

- Putting a sensitive document in a safe
- Encrypting or digitally signing a sensitive file
- Ensuring that multiple instances of a service are available for use
- Having two or more individuals assigned to a role in case one goes on vacation
- Limiting the number of principals which have administrative authority over a system or component
- Hard drive encryption

Protection strategies focused on information in-transit address risks associated with information traveling between different components within the system, between systems, or between the system and a client. Examples of protection strategies for information in-transit include:

- Using a screen protector to limit who can see information displayed on a monitor
- Using SSL or VPN encryption for network traffic
- Use of tamper evident tape on a package
- Implementing a security checkpoint prior to allowing entry into a secure facility
- Use of a firewall or proxy server to inspect and control network communication

The third state of information occurs when it is in use. This state of information is perhaps the most difficult to protect because, in many cases, protections implemented around information at-rest or in-transit must be removed to allow for processing.

For example, while a safe might protect a sensitive document from theft during storage it should be expected that someone will open the safe, remove the document, and use it legitimately. The document remains unprotected during this period, which is the case with most forms of information.

A similar example occurs when an encrypted file is decrypted for use by the application. During this time, the unencrypted information is likely exposed to system memory or possibly even displayed on the monitor.

Protecting information while it is in use is a challenge, thus many of the defenses revolve around limiting the amount of time information remains in this state and limiting exposure. In some cases, software systems can process encrypted data without decryption. Examples of protection strategies for information in-use include:

- Using a screen protector to limit visibility of a computer monitor
- Enforcing rules around discussing sensitive information outside protected spaces
- Avoiding writing decrypted information derived from an encrypted source to disk
- Partitioning the system to isolate processing of encrypted data using virtualization or application containers
- Reducing the amount of time an encrypted file remains decrypted in memory

Protecting Confidentiality

To protect confidentiality, we must ensure that sensitive information is only made available to those individuals, systems, and components which are authorized to read it. This sounds simple on the surface, but as you begin to analyze how a system operates you are likely to find a variety of unintended opportunities that might allow an unauthorized individual or application to read confidentiality sensitive information.

The Bell–LaPadula Model

In November 1973, the MITRE Corporation (a large nonprofit organization commonly involved with US government research) released a document titled "Secure Computer Systems: Mathematical Foundations" (Bell & LaPadula, 1973). This document contained a mathematical model developed by D. Elliott Bell and Leonard J. LaPadula which can be used to validate a system's ability to protect confidentiality. This algorithm is based on the concept of a system which handles information of differing levels of confidentiality without exposure of higher sensitivity information to lower sensitivity processes or files.

The Bell–LaPadula model describes three properties which a system must abide by to protect confidentiality sensitive information:

- Information of a higher classification must not be readable by any entity operating at a lower security classification.
- Information of a higher classification must not write to any entity operating at a lower security classification.
- A discretionary access control list should identify principals which have authorization to set or change the classification of information processed by the system.

The first two properties in this model are focusing on a mandatory access control (MAC) system – a system where security is applied using defined levels. These levels apply to the confidentiality sensitivity of information. While the system is designed to describe a very strict linear approach to protection, the underlying concepts behind the formulas can be used to describe protection of confidentiality between any two components, systems, sessions, or any other situation whereby we need to protect the confidentiality of sensitive information from exposure.

No Read Up   The first property of the Bell–LaPadula model can be simplified to the term "no read up". In other words, a system or component operating at a lower confidentiality protection level should not be able to access or include information of a higher confidentiality sensitivity level. This also means that a document must be classified on the basis of the highest confidentiality sensitivity information it contains, which follows the logic from our previous chapter.

Common failures of the "no read up" policy include:

- Lax read permissions on a file server or other content sharing service
- Intentionally saving confidential information with insufficient protections to enable unauthorized sharing
- Inadvertently discussing sensitive information in a conference room where unapproved individuals are present
- Allowing an application to read sensitive operating system information without proper authorization (also known as an information disclosure vulnerability)

No Write Down   Our second property states that information of a higher confidentiality sensitivity should not be written to an area of lower confidentiality protection. This aspect prevents the system from inadvertently exposing sensitive information by writing it to unprotected locations.

Common failures of the "no write down" policy include:

- A system or component which is processing confidential information writing an unencrypted version of the information to a temporary file
- An individual saving administrative credentials to a file
- Writing your password on a sticky note and placing it under your keyboard
- Checking in code containing credentials to a source code repository

- Saving sensitive information to a personal drive
- Intentionally disclosing sensitive information to unapproved individuals
- Sharing a credential with an unauthorized user

The Star Security Property   The third property identifies the need for discretionary access to set or change the level of any information handled by the system. Principals with this authorization can configure (and potentially circumvent) security of the system; therefore, any principal with this authorization would be considered administrative.

Examples of failures of this principle include:

- Using administrative authority to intentionally change an access control list to allow reading of confidential data or writing to unauthorized locations
- Intentionally lowering the sensitivity of a confidentiality sensitive document
- Changing an access control list to grant unauthorized principals administrative authorization to a confidentiality sensitive system or component

Example of a Confidentiality Breach

Imagine you have an individual who is working on a press release for your company. Press releases are public once released; therefore, there should be no confidential information included in this document. We would have a problem if the individual had access to confidential information and included sensitive strategic information to create the document.

To identify which property of the Bell–LaPadula model was violated we must understand the root cause of the security failure. Possible causes include:

- The sensitive information was not properly classified (failure of identification)
- The individual had the ability to read a document they weren't supposed to (failure of the no read-up property)

- The individual knowingly wrote confidentiality sensitive information into a press release (failure of the no write-down property)
- The individual had administrative authority and used it to change the sensitivity of the document (failure of the star security property)
- The individual had administrative authority and used it to change security protections for the confidentiality sensitive document (failure of the star security property)

Protecting Confidentiality Using Access Controls

An access control can be used to block the ability to read confidentiality sensitive information. These techniques constrain exposure of the information within a defined edge, such as a secure room or facility.

At the most basic level, confidentiality can be protected by isolating the system by design. This approach is best when there is no legitimate utility for access to confidential information over a specific form of access. For example:

- Intentionally not developing or exposing a software interface that allows read from a low confidentiality process to a high confidentiality area, or write from a high confidentiality process to a low confidentiality area
- Using a screen protector to prevent others from viewing what is displayed on your monitor
- Using hardware engineering to enforce one-way communication by design (i.e., designing a transmit only medium from a system handling information of lower confidentiality to one handling higher confidentiality sensitivity information)
- Using a Faraday cage or TEMPEST design to limit RF emissions
- Only allowing access in specific conditions, such as using a wall that only allows entry through a specific area
- Using a white noise generator to prevent unauthorized individuals from listening in on sensitive conversations
- Using a write blocker or nonpersistent virtual desktop infrastructure (VDI) solution to prevent storing of confidential information

Protecting Confidentiality Using Access Controls
Paired With Authorization Controls

Access controls paired with an authorization control are a slightly more capable approach to defending confidentiality. Using this approach, We can reduce exposure to only a subset of authenticated individuals.

Many systems gravitate toward this method due to its simplicity and flexibility. While effective, it is important to remember that this method of protection is likely insufficient from an assume breach perspective, thus Highly sensitive information will likely require additional protection.

Examples of this approach include:

- Using organizational policy to prevent disclosure of confidentiality sensitive strategic information broadly (i.e., need to know or facility security clearance requirements)
- Using a firewall paired with a virtual private network (VPN) to require authentication prior to access
- Having a security guard at the entrance to your building to prevent unauthorized access
- Installing badge authenticated turnstiles or badge access doors to prevent unauthorized individuals from entering confidentiality sensitive areas

Protecting Confidentiality Using Authorization Controls on Information

The most effective solution for protecting confidentiality is to implement an authorization control on the information itself. This strategy is especially effective because the information will remain protected even when it leaves the system.

Encryption and obfuscation are really the only true authorization controls which can be applied directly to information.

Obfuscation uses obscure information encoding or delivery to protect the information from discovery. With this technique, the information is encoded in some sort of scheme which causes it to be unrecognizable to the naked eye.

For example, steganography can be used to hide confidential information within an image. This approach is effective until an analyst

identifies the semi-random pattern and develops a process of extract-
ing the information from the image. Other examples of obfuscation
include:

- Using a dead drop technique to deliver information to a spy
- Hiding information in a document using invisible ink
- Encoding information by replacing letters or binary informa-
  tion using an obscure algorithm
- Hiding a safe code by using secret words or patterns which
  require the reader to know a decoding algorithm

Encryption, on the other hand, produces a highly random output
which cannot be decoded without the associated decryption key.
This forces an attacker to use a brute force attack against the
key itself (or find a vulnerability in the algorithm or encryption
process).

The main difference between obfuscation and encryption is the use
of a cryptographic key. Obfuscated information typically requires no
credential to decode, whereas encryption does. If implemented properly, an encrypted message should not be breakable by an attacker
within a reasonable amount of time. Unfortunately, good encryption
is only feasibly performed using technology, rendering us dependent
on the technology realm for this protection.

Information encrypted with a trustworthy algorithm and suffi-
ciently protected keys should be able to be placed in an untrustworthy location with limited risk. Other strategies rely on access
controls and proper data handling, whereas encryption provides
defense so long as the decryption key remains protected. In other
words, the algorithm is the domain and the decryption key is the
credential.

Examples of using encryption to protect information include:

- Using digital rights management to hide the contents of a
  document
- SSL encryption used when talking to servers over a network
- VPN encryption
- Drive or volume encryption
- The enigma machine from World War II

Protecting Integrity

To protect integrity, we need to prevent unauthorized changes in information stored or processed by the system. When unauthorized changes occur, we should have a mechanism to detect them. In many ways, protecting integrity means controlling write authorization and ensuring information read by the system for decision-making is trustworthy.

The principles used to protect system integrity are in many ways the opposite of those used to protect confidentiality. While the approach may differ, many systems and components will implement both protections over the same information. This is a great example of where we need to understand what type of risk we need to defend against when designing our security solution.

The Biba Integrity Model

In June 1975, Mitre published a state machine model designed by Kenneth J. Biba (Mitre Corporation, 1975). This model focused on protecting the integrity of a system by preventing unauthorized writes to high integrity information and ensuring that information processed by the system came from a trustworthy source.

Information in the Biba model is separated into different integrity levels. High integrity information must remain reliable and accurate at all costs because a failure of integrity could be catastrophic. For example:

- The configuration of systems involved with critical decisions such as the navigation component in a self-driving car
- Authenticity of a letter directing military action
- The applications allowed to run on an enterprise authentication system
- Trustworthiness of a GPS signal used in maritime navigation
- A database containing user accounts and credentials for enterprise authentication

Biba's model outlines three rules which a system must abide by to protect high integrity information:

- The simple integrity property which states that a system operating at a higher level should not reference information at a lower level during its operation

- The star integrity property which states that a system operating at a lower level should be unable to write information to a system operating at a higher level
- The invocation property which states that a system at a lower integrity level cannot request a higher integrity level

Once again, while the concepts in the Biba model are written specifically to describe how a software application is designed to operate, we will focus on the essence of the concept to enable its application to systems in a broader sense.

No Read Down   Our first property states that a system processing high integrity information should not reference lower integrity information during processing. Stated differently, the integrity of a system will be limited by the lowest integrity information used during processing.

Imagine you have a bouncer outside of your night club checking ID cards to ensure everyone who enters is of legal age. Most bouncers will only accept a government ID card for this purpose; therefore, the level of trust you might have in your policy is derived from the integrity of the organization issuing the ID cards (and the ability to detect a forged credential).

Later on, you decide to also accept letters from the individual's mom as a form of authentication (this would be a trust). Despite the issues with validating the authenticity of the credential, your system is now only as integral as the lowest integrity mom. In other words, you are likely to have poor integrity in your policy's enforcement and therefore more underage individuals in your night club.

Common failures of the no read down policy include:

- Trusting an untrustworthy partner for authentication
- Failure to validate the integrity of information received by the system (i.e., signal spoofing)
- Failure to validate the integrity of information used in a critical service or component
- Accepting weak authentication to a system which otherwise requires strong authentication
- Using a rumor or speculation to make an important decision
- Psychological operations

No Write Up The second property states that a process operating at a lower integrity should not be able to write information to high integrity processes or information – or, for short, no write up.

This property is designed to ensure that high integrity information is not corrupted or colored by low integrity inferences, thus ensuring its continued integrity.

A real-world example of the "no write up" policy occurs on social media daily. Many treat social media as a source of interaction with our friends and family. In addition, we tend to subscribe to various personal interests (either intentionally or through profiling and targeted advertising). Unfortunately, most things on social media lack journalistic integrity and result in false information being repeated or "reshared" by individuals without validation. This condition commonly results in a higher integrity source (a friend or family member) repeating untrustworthy information. By resharing low integrity information as themselves they have ultimately violated the "no write up" policy.

Other examples of violations of the "no write up" property include:

- News sources publishing articles based on unvalidated rumors
- Loading information into a system or component from a corrupted data source
- Domain fronting (when a trusted public DNS domain allows content from unvalidated subdomains to be associated as subdomains of their trusted domain name)
- Results of a 51% attack in a blockchain network

The Invocation Property Our third property states that systems operating at a lower tier should not be able to tamper with the kernel, which is the component enforcing the integrity rules. The kernel is essentially our reference monitor and translates to our concept of a domain. Restated, the integrity of the system's operations is only as trustworthy as the integrity of the domain; therefore, any administrative authorization which grants the ability to tamper with domain decisions must be protected from low integrity systems, components, and principals.

This is perhaps one of the most violated principals in system design when we talk about administrative authorization. Think of a corporate computer. This system may be charged with protecting sensitive company information, credentials, and a variety of other sensitive assets. The integrity of this system can be ensured so long as administrative authority is limited, and vulnerabilities are mitigated or patched.

Unfortunately, in practice it is common to grant excessive administrative authority to reduce support call volume or speed up service implementation. Each time we grant administrative authority to a principal, we run the risk of losing system integrity.

Other examples of violation of the invocation property include:

- Bypassing normal security protocol due to emergency circumstances (perceived or real)
- Failing to perform a background check on an employee in a key position
- Failure to validate the authenticity of a software application prior to launch or installation
- Elevation of privilege exploits
- Performing actions based on a phishing e-mail or social engineering call

Example of an Integrity Breach

One common example of an integrity breach is a phishing attack. In these cases, the individual fails to properly authenticate an email or other message and performs an action based on misplaced trust. The impact of the breach depends on the instructions that were followed.

For example, the attacker may be able to establish illegitimate access and authorization to the computer if the malware provides remote control. This would be an example of access and authorization by proxy leading to an integrity impact on the computer. The malware may then download other malicious code and install it on the computer to provide durable control over the system.

Using the Biba model we can dissect this incident into its various parts:

- The user provided trust without properly authenticating the attacker (failure of authentication)
- The user proxied the attacker's email access to access to their user session by executing the malware (no write up)

- If the user had administrative authority over the computer, they may have also impacted the integrity of the system itself (failure of the invocation property)
- The malware downloaded and installed additional malicious code onto the computer from an untrusted source (no read down)

Protecting Integrity Using Access Controls

Our first option to protect the integrity of a system involves using an access control. Access controls are an effective way of preventing a system and its components from connecting to known low-reputation sources. This option is also useful when individuals or traffic must be forwarded through a checkpoint to verify integrity or to detect malicious content.

Access controls are commonly used in the physical world to force individuals through checkpoints to detect contraband or illegal behavior, such as:

- Checkpoints which identify individuals driving under the influence of alcohol
- Use of metal detectors to identify weapons upon entry into a government building
- Being frisked or patted down before entering a concert

In the technology world, one example of this strategy involves using a firewall or proxy server to constrain access to approved destinations. The Internet is a considerably untrustworthy environment. Some security-minded organizations explicitly block access from servers to all Internet sites. Others use threat intelligence to explicitly block access to network destinations known to be used by attackers. This approach can be helpful in reducing unnecessary risk to important systems.

Using a proxy server is also an example of using an access control to funnel traffic to low integrity sources through a trusted checkpoint where it can be inspected for malicious content.

Other examples of using access controls to protect integrity include:

- Using a write blocker to protect the integrity of a disk under forensic examination

- Using a physical cable as opposed to wireless networking to facilitate communication between high integrity systems
- Performing a criminal background check or drug test as part of the hiring process
- Explicitly designing a system or its components to protect integrity by not exposing access
- Writing log data to a write once read many (WORM) storage medium
- Using tamper-evident tape to seal a sensitive letter or box

Unfortunately, this protection strategy does not afford any protection to the information outside of the system. For example, there would be no way to know if someone were to take high integrity information outside of the system, modify it, and try to present it as legitimate.

Protecting Integrity Using Access Controls Paired With Authorization Controls

Using an authorization control paired with an access control enables us to be selective over which principals are allowed access to integrity sensitive interfaces. As a result, this approach is ideal when you have information which is only needed for a subset of authenticated individuals or systems.

A physical world example of an access control paired with an authorization control would be an airport security checkpoint. This enables authentication in addition to screening. For example, airport security checks the identity of the individual and validates whether they have a legitimate reason to enter. This check costs additional time, but ultimately helps improve the safety of travel.

A common example of this technique in the virtual world involves protecting administrative interfaces by placing them behind a firewall and using a VPN. The firewall prevents any inbound network connections, whereas the VPN allows authenticated and trusted individuals to access these internal network interfaces.

Other examples of using this protection strategy include:

- Enforcing authentication on a web portal before granting access to integrity sensitive documents
- A security guard checking ID cards at a building entrance

- Using a safe to protect integrity sensitive documents
- IPSec in Authenticated Header (AH) mode
- Chain of custody tracking forms used with tamper proof evidence bags

As with other access protections, the integrity of information cannot be guaranteed once it leaves the system.

Protecting Integrity Using Authorization Controls on the Information

The most effective solution is to apply an authorization control to the information itself. This approach enables integrity to be validated both inside and outside the bounds of the system. Unfortunately, once again our most effective solutions exist solely in the technology world due to advanced mathematical algorithms.

Signatures have been long considered an effective integrity check in the human process world. This integrity check is considered acceptable for checks, credit cards, loan applications, and a variety of other important documents. Unfortunately, forgeries are rather simple to create and signatures are difficult to authenticate accurately. Because of this, trust in signatures as a form of authentication and integrity validation might be somewhat misplaced.

In the digital world, the most common authorization control used to protect the integrity of information is the digital signature. A digital signature is a cryptographic hash of information which is then encrypted using a key, enabling us to change our strategy from performing an integrity check to performing an authenticity check. This means we can trust that a specific principal created the content and that it hasn't changed since creation up to our confidence in the encryption key's confidentiality, and both the hash algorithm and encryption algorithm's integrity.

Examples of using an authorization control to protect the integrity of information include:

- Authenticode signatures
- S/MIME email signatures
- Digitally signed documents

- Smart card authentication (such as the Kerberos PKINIT protocol)
- Authentication performed during SSL
- PKI Certificate chaining

Protecting Availability

Protecting availability means ensuring that the service and its information are accessible for legitimate use. In many ways, ensuring availability means controlling "delete" authorization performed within the service. We achieve this through redundancy, scalability, and recoverability.

An attack against availability can be equally crippling as attacks against confidentiality or integrity. Ransomware, bombing, denial of service, assassination, and military blockades are just some examples of highly effective strategies which target crippling resource availability. Many of these conditions can be recovered from with proper planning.

Redundancy

The redundancy of a system, component, or its information refers to the number of instances which are maintained to accommodate for failure. Redundancy ensures that another entity is available if one or more component failures occur.

For a component to be considered truly redundant, it must be capable of accepting the full load of another component in the event of a failure. This typically means having additional components waiting on standby for use, or spreading the load between all components, but limiting the throughput such that a component failure can be handled without an outage.

The "n" System Scalability is planned using the "n" system, where "n" represents the number of resources required for normal operation. We use this to describe the throughput capacity in relative terms to ensure that we understand the number of failures which can be accounted for.

For example, if our service required three widgets for normal operation and we purchased four widgets in case one failed we would have $n + 1$ redundancy. In the same light, if we had six widgets for the same service, we would have $2n$ redundancy.

Fault Domains A fault domain represents the maximum area of impact for a single failure. This term is commonly used to describe datacenters that guarantee power, network connectivity, and cooling on a per-rack basis. In other words, each individual rack has its necessary resources even if the one next to it may have failed.

When planning for redundancy, it is important to ensure that our redundant resources are not all within the same fault domain. In other words, the system and its components need to have an independent dedicated path to any of their dependent resources such that a failure of one will not impact the others.

Georedundancy Another consideration when planning for redundancy is georedundancy. Georedundancy means that resources exist in different geographic regions such that a failure in one location does not impact service delivery – they simply are delivered from another location.

Georedundancy is crucial when planning for major catastrophic events such as fires, hurricanes, earthquakes, or other events which impact a large geographical area. When planning for georedundancy, always ensure that georedundant locations are far enough away such that a major catastrophic event in one area will not impact the other(s).

Scalability

Scalability is the ability for a system or component to increase capacity as demand increases. This aspect of system design ensures that services remain available in the event of either a spike in usage or a denial-of-service attack.

Think of a sports stadium. Many sports stadiums have multiple entrances to let fans in. Some events may not require the ability to handle the maximum volume of fans, therefore many of the gates may be unmanned to save on costs. Because of its design, the stadium remains able to increase its fan throughput by opening the additional gates. While this increases the operational cost of the stadium, the increase in revenue from ticket sales greatly outweighs the cost for the additional staff.

Technology once again provides the best example of high availability design. Properly designed applications can signal their throughput, either through raw resource utilization such as CPU, memory, disk I/O, or network throughput, or through custom telemetry providers implemented during development. This information can be monitored to determine when a component approaches capacity and can signal deployment of additional instances.

When designing a system for scalability, be sure to understand any limitations which may occur as the system scales out (adds additional instances) or scales up (adds additional resources to an existing instance). For example, the database for a website may have plenty of resources with five webservers but may near its capacity when 25 instances are deployed. Be sure to define acceptable limits for your application and test these limits where possible.

Another consideration when designing a system for scalability is the ability to scale in (eliminate instances of a component) or scale down (reduce resources for a component). Scaling in or down enables you to reduce operational cost when increased capability is no longer necessary. Additionally, designing a system to scale in implies the ability to eliminate an instance on demand, which can be used to respond to an attack more rapidly.

Recoverability

Our third aspect of a highly available system is its recoverability. Put simply, recoverability is the ability for a system to handle component failures gracefully. This aspect is what enables seamless scalability and redundancy without causing outages or failures due to corrupt information, dropped sessions, or other service issues.

In the human process world, recoverability means ensuring that a system remains operational when individuals involved in the system take vacation, get sick, resign, or are otherwise unavailable. For senior leadership roles, proactive succession planning can be used to delegate roles which accept responsibility for the missing individual until they return or are replaced. This helps reduce the impact associated with sudden nonavailability and ensures that important decisions and activities are not accidentally missed.

In the technology world, recoverability is mostly a software design concept. Each component involved in the software system should be designed to become unavailable without warning with little or no impact to service operation. This includes the ability to recover from partially written or processed information.

The ACID Test   In 1983, engineers Andreas Reuter and Theo Haerder published a paper titled "Principles of Transaction-Oriented Database Recovery" with the Association for Computing Machinery. This paper described the properties which are required for a reliable fault-tolerant database using the acronym ACID (Haerder & Reuter, 1983). ACID stands for:

- Atomicity: The system must not commit partial transactions – it must commit all or nothing of any transaction.
- Consistency: Each transaction must commit only legal results per the software system's specification.
- Isolation: All transactions occurring within the system must run separately from other concurrent transactions.
- Durability: We must be able to trust that a completed transaction has been properly committed to permanent storage.

While this paper was published about databases, these concepts remain true for all aspects of a recoverable system. Any request made by a user of a reliable system should pass the ACID test to ensure information is not lost in the event of an outage.

Protecting Authorization Control

There are many benefits to leveraging authorization control over access control, but those benefits come at a risk. An authorization control system is only as good as it is secure. In other words, remember that the components involved in authorization control hold the keys to system security.

Going back to our diagram about the concepts of authorization control, we can discern that the security value of a domain is essentially the sum total of all authorizations it can grant to securables plus the value of all principals it can authenticate. If other domains trust this domain for principal authentication, we can also add the value of any authorizations that trusting domains grant to those principals. Because of this, the authorization control aspect of a system is typically the most important aspect of protection.

Protecting the authorization control aspect of your system means applying the CIA triad to the five principles of authorization control. This results in 15 aspects which need to be protected to ensure security. These protections can be grouped into three general categories:

- Protections that guarantee the integrity of the authorization control system
- Protections that guarantee operational confidentiality of the authorization control system
- Protections that guarantee availability of the authorization control system

Protection of confidentiality and availability is fairly straightforward; thus, we won't be diving into specifics of their implementation. Protecting integrity of the authorization control system is perhaps the most challenging and impactful. Integrity is also what directly translates to the trust you can put in authorization control. Because of this, let's dive into what it means to protect integrity in-depth.

Protecting Domain Integrity

As the component which both authenticates principals and controls access to securables, the domain is the most important aspect of an authorization control system to protect. Loss of integrity of a domain means inability to trust decisions made by the authorization control system, thus inability to trust the system itself.

Protecting integrity of the domain involves two main elements: ensuring that we trust any components used within the domain and limiting any administrative authority to the domain.

To ensure that we trust components used within the domain, we must ensure that each component used within the domain is both trusted and validated. Any ability to add an untrusted component into the domain undermines the security of all authentication and authorization operations performed by the domain. This means:

- Any individuals involved in performing security operations should have a background check
- Software used within domain should come from a trusted source and be validated
- Components used within the domain should be stored in a write-protected location
- The domain should only reference trustworthy data for performing its operations

Limiting administrative authorization to the domain limits the possibility of tamper. Any principal with administrative authorization to the domain can circumvent protections, thereby enabling them to load unauthorized components. Any principal with authorization which can impact the integrity of the domain should be highly protected (i.e., strong credentials, limited exposure, and time-limited authorization).

Protecting Trust Integrity

Trusts offer an opportunity for an attacker to tamper with the authentication aspect of the domain's operation. Any time a trust is implemented, authenticity becomes reduced to the integrity of the least trusted domain. For this reason, trusts should only be made with higher integrity sources of authentication.

The ability to create or modify a trust should also be considered administrative authority to the domain. This type of authorization can be used to undermine the overall trust of the domain, thereby potentially allowing an untrustworthy data source to convey authentication which may grant authorization to illegitimate entities.

Protecting Membership Integrity

The security value of membership is derived from the sum of all authorizations granted to a given group. In other words, the value of protecting membership will vary depending on what that membership grants authorization to. For example, membership that enables you to read low sensitivity information is significantly less valuable than membership which grants administrative authorization.

We should protect the integrity of membership in the same way that we protect the security of anything which that membership grants authorization to. This means that membership which grants administrative authorization should be protected disproportionately greater than membership which does not. Additionally, authorization which grants permission to read confidentiality sensitive information, write to integrity sensitive information, or delete availability sensitive information should be protected at the level associated with the information it grants authorization to.

Membership that grants sensitive authorization should always be maintained by the domain where the authorization is granted or a higher integrity domain. Trusting a lower integrity domain with membership that can resolve to administrative authority reduces the overall trust in authorization decisions made by the domain.

Ensuring Principal Integrity

Principal integrity is the confidence that the individual, service, or component that is authenticated is the intended entity. In other words, this translates to confidence that only intended entities are using their assigned security principals – and not an illegitimate individual.

Principal integrity is derived not only from the entity controlling the principal itself but also from the confidence derived from their credential strength, exposure, and integrity. This causes principal integrity to be one of the most complex aspects of protecting your authorization system.

Credential Issuance   Principal integrity begins with process used to issue credentials. The authenticity of a principal comes from the confidence that only intended individuals or resources assigned to use the credential have or can produce it. Confidence is reduced any time an individual or resource other than the intended user is aware of a credential. This is further reduced if the credential is stored in a medium readable by other individuals or services as part of issuance.

Always perform strong authentication during initial credential issuance. The type of authentication performed will vary depending on the type of resource being assigned the credential and may differ depending on the authorization granted to the associated principal.

Let's look at some examples of low integrity credential issuance processes:

- Using a standard or predictable initial password for users can enable unauthorized individuals to guess credentials for new or unused accounts
- Having a representative set an initial credential means that someone other than the intended principal knows the new account's credential
- Transmitting a credential in email can enable an attacker with access to the user's mailbox to masquerade using their principal
- Failure to perform a proper background check on an individual prior to credential issuance can lead to malicious or untrustworthy individuals controlling a valid principal
- Lack of network encryption during identity provisioning may enable an attacker to intercept the credential

Principal Integrity Principal integrity refers to the ongoing trust in authentication after credential issuance. In other words, ensuring we maintain trust that the entity using a principal is the intended entity. Since a principal is identified by one or more sets of credentials, this protection relies on ensuring that the authenticity of those credentials remains intact.

The ability to either add or change a credential assigned to a principal without knowing the current credential undermines principal integrity. However, this capability is necessary in most authorization control systems. This ability is commonly granted to individuals and systems involved with account maintenance, such as password reset functions, badge issuance, and help desk personnel.

The ability to set or add a credential for an individual should be limited where possible, and any principal with that ability should be considered at the same sensitivity level at a minimum. Principals with this authorization should be treated as administrative credentials as they can circumvent normal security procedures.

Credential Confidentiality   Perhaps the most impactful aspect of principal integrity is credential confidentiality, an attribute derived from its exposure. Any time a credential is transmitted, saved, or processed in memory it runs the risk of compromise, and anyone with read access to where the credential is stored or processed has the opportunity to compromise its confidentiality, thereby compromising the integrity of the principal which it authenticates.

Following the Bell–LaPadula model for confidentiality, we should avoid storing credentials where other principals have read authorization and ensure credentials are not written to unsecure locations. Practices such as maintaining a password list on a personal computer, writing a password on a sticky note, or sharing credentials with coworkers are all examples of credential confidentiality risks.

In addition, the use of asymmetric authentication can help improve credential confidentiality. Asymmetric authentication uses a cryptographic relationship between two keys instead of a centralized database of credentials or their derivatives. By using asymmetric authentication, we avoid risks associated with theft of the credential database.

Avoid using reusable authentication protocols where possible, such as basic or hash authentication. Where possible, leverage challenge response authentication protocols to help ensure that credentials are not reusable.

Finally, consider using credential translation to issue session credentials for subsequent authentication. This helps protect the confidentiality of the original credential by replacing it with a less powerful session-specific credential.

Examples of credential confidentiality protection strategies include:

- Storing credentials in purpose-built authentication devices where possible (i.e., TPM, HSM, smart card, smart RFID)
- Using challenge–response protocols where possible to avoid exposure of the credential itself
- Leveraging asymmetric or one-time credentials instead of symmetric credentials

- Ensuring encryption is enforced anytime authentication occurs
- Ensuring any component which performs authentication is shielded from read access by other components

Credential Strength Our ability to trust the authenticity of a principal is also derived from the strength of any credential which can be used in its authentication. Weak or predictable credentials provide an attacker the opportunity to guess the associated credential, thereby undermining our trust in the entity authenticating as the principal.

Where possible, avoid use of human-created credentials as they tend to be simple, predictable, and memorable. Where this is necessary, leverage a form of proxy authentication by enabling the user to authenticate to a locally accessible device (such as a TPM, HSM, or smart card) to unlock use of a stronger and less predictable credential for authentication to public-facing services.

Another way to improve credential strength is through use of multifactor authentication. This requires multiple individual credentials from different sources to establish authentication, thus greatly increasing the effort required by an attacker to establish a new session as the principal.

Credential Validity Period Where possible, avoid use of credentials with long validity periods to increase confidence in principal integrity. Credentials with a longer validity period run a greater risk of being stolen or compromised leading to increased risk of compromise, and thereby reduced trust in principal integrity.

Credential Revocation Over time credentials will be stolen, lost, exposed, or compromised for one reason or another. When this occurs, it is important to have the ability to revoke the credential so that it can no longer be accepted for valid authentication. As a result, the ability to revoke compromised credentials directly translates to your ability to trust the integrity of principal in the event of credential compromise.

Revocation works best in the technology world. While you can publish a list of stolen ID cards to a guard, it is likely to be much less effective than blocking the credential from being used for authentication in a software system.

Authenticating Domain Integrity   When using trusts, the integrity of a principal is only as good as the integrity of the domain where it was authenticated. A trust outsources authentication to an external domain, therefore any principals authenticated by a trusted domain cannot be more trustworthy than the domain itself. This is especially important if the principal is granted either administrative authorization or authorization to sensitive information.

Avoid granting administrative authorization to principals authenticated by a trusted domain unless that trusted domain is considered higher integrity than where it has administrative authority. If a trusted domain is compromised, any principal with administrative authority in the trusting domain can be used to spread the compromise to the trusting domain.

Protecting Securable Integrity

Our final aspect of ensuring integrity of our authorization system pertains to securables. A securable's integrity is derived from any authorization granted to it. As a result, protecting the securable means ensuring control over any sensitive nonadministrative authorization or administrative authorization granted to a principal.

Protecting Administrative Authorization   Administrative authorization should only be granted based on controls within the system itself. In other words, we must ensure that the system does not derive administrative authorization based on factors outside of the system, such as groups sourced from a trusted domain.

Any time administrative authorization is delegated to an external entity we run the risk of compromise of the trusted system leading to a compromise of a trusting system. Groups are typically used to design administrative roles within the system, but the association with that group should be derived from within the system's boundary to limit the impact of credential compromise.

For the highest value systems, consider using a separate domain solely for administrative authorization to the service. This approach helps reduce credential exposure outside the system, thus reducing the risk of credential theft. Additionally, this design isolates the impact of a security breach by ensuring that principals with administrative authority in one area are of no value to other systems.

Time-Limited Authorization   All sensitive or administrative authorization to a securable should be time-limited where possible. The amount of time that authorization remains valid should be derived from the level of risk that it poses to the security of the system or organization as a whole.

The first method of establishing time-limited authorization is ensuring sensitive authorization is reviewed periodically. Periodic review ensures that principals do not continually gain authorization throughout their lifetime and that authorization is removed when it is no longer necessary. Where possible, enforcing oversight in this process (such as including managerial review and approval of requests to extend authorization) can help reduce risk.

Our second category of time-limited authorization pertains to administrative authorization. This form of authorization is typically not needed for routine tasks and can be requested on-demand. In the technology world, this is referred to as privileged access management, or PAM.

In a PAM solution, when a principal needs administrative authorization to a securable it can request that authority on a temporary basis. If approved, authorization is granted for a short period of time (a few hours in many cases) before it returns to a nonadministrative state. These requests typically follow an approval process, are logged, and are only available to a small subset of user principals which are reviewed regularly using our process for time-limited authorization.

Access Control List Integrity   As previously mentioned, the integrity of a securable is only as good as its access control list. Any principal with the ability to edit the access control list for a securable should be considered at the same integrity level as the object the access control list protects.

Risk-Based Authorization Control

Imagine you are working at a security desk and someone approaches with their ID card. Everything about the authentication seems to be valid, but they are acting suspiciously. As a security guard you might consider asking additional questions or block their ability to enter altogether depending on the situation. This is an example of risk-based authorization control.

Risk-based authorization control is a technique where otherwise legitimate authorization might require additional authentication or limit authorization based on circumstances surrounding the authentication or authorization request. Conditions might include one or more of the following:

- Attempt to perform a highly sensitive action, such as transfer of a large amount of money or access to sensitive information
- Recent suspicious activity associated with the principal, such as a brute force authentication attack or authentication from a rare or geodistant location
- Risk level associated with the system or component performing the authentication or authorization request, such as a recent malware detection or known vulnerable component

The Process of Creating and Maintaining a Secure System

Security needs to be designed and developed alongside the system's architecture to be effective. Bolting security onto the outside of an existing system should be a strategy of necessity as it adds complexity, increases operational expenditure, and results in less overall security.

Imagine you were handed an inherently weak military emplacement and were asked to secure it without changing any of its internals. Sure, you could add weaponry, stronger or taller fencing, or add gate guards, but at some point, it still needs to be accessible for legitimate use. All of the bolted-on security makes legitimate use challenging, and all of it falls apart if an attacker can call someone on the inside and trick them into emailing sensitive documents or escorting in an attacker because of poor vetting.

Over time, the threat landscape will change and cause the need to update the system's posture. This is especially true in the technology world, but also exists in the physical world as well as the human process world. This drives the need for a living process to continually review and update our system.

Microsoft's Security Development Lifecycle

Michael Howard and David LeBlanc published the popular book "Writing Secure Code" in November of 2001 which later led to the establishment of Microsoft's Security Development Lifecycle (SDL). While this process focuses heavily on secure software design, many of the core concepts are universal and can be applied to the creation, maintenance, and decommission of a service and its components.

Microsoft's SDL is broken down into 12 practices which are designed to reduce the number and severity of vulnerabilities in software. This leads to improved compliance, security assurance, and a reduction in the cost of rework. We will use these principals to structure our discussion, but their content will be adapted to fit the concepts used in this book. As a result, this section may deviate somewhat from their official guidance.

Provide Training

Training is a crucial component in successful implementation of any security program. There are three main categories of training that an organization should invest in to protect their sensitive information and systems:

- User training
- Administrator training
- Developer or architect training

User Training Anyone involved with a system that handles sensitive information should receive regular training on its proper handling. Employees and partners shouldn't be expected to understand the risk, value, and impact of information within the system without training.

Additionally, users need to understand the protections expected of them for each type of information classification they may encounter. Ideally, this training should be performed regularly (many organizations perform this annually).

User training should focus on topics such as:

- The risks of information mishandling
- Phishing and social engineering
- Essential Elements of Friendly Information (EEFI)
- The different classifications of information they may encounter and their associated protections
- Processes for reporting a security incident

Note that all users (including administrators, developers, and architects) should receive user training.

Administrator Training   Your administrators are the individuals with the power to circumvent security, thus it is crucial that they understand the risks and expectations of doing so. From an operational perspective, individuals with administrative authorization are your primary defense against vulnerability.

Administrator training should focus on topics such as:

- The risk of misconfiguration
- The impact of granting excessive authorization
- Lax security practices
- Proper change control
- Common post-breach attack techniques

Developer or Architect Training   Developers and architects are the ones responsible for ensuring that components within the system as well as the system itself operate reliably and securely. The attack landscape is always changing, thus it is crucial that developers and architects understand new attack techniques and the mistakes that lead to them.

Developer and architect training are likely to be a lot more technical than other forms of training, focusing on topics such as:

- Newly identified attacks or vulnerabilities in system components

- Authentication weaknesses and attacks
- Flaws in component design and how to detect them
- Proper development process and the SDL

Define Security Requirements

Security requirements are as important as other component design requirements in SDL. These requirements should be derived from the protections prescribed when we defined the risk of compromise during identification.

Security requirements should also be reasonable. While adding additional security requirements may sound like a good idea during design, in practice this increases the time to delivery and usually increases the overhead associated with operation. In addition, there is also the opportunity cost associated with developing other capabilities instead of a security capability.

As part of development, ensure that test cases are built to validate these security requirements. While this is usually considered a software concept, tests should be performed on physical and human process systems and components as well. Testing validates the protection of components within the system and training needs for individuals.

Define Metrics and Compliance Reporting

While they meet occasionally, compliance does not imply security. Because of this, metrics may need to be implemented within the system to simplify compliance reporting. Implementing these metrics during design will reduce cost associated with future compliance audits, ultimately reducing the overhead of operations.

Perform Threat Modeling

Threat modeling is the process of mapping out access provided or used by the system. Each available form of access, whether it be component to component, component to dependency, or client to component, comes with its own potential risk. Knowing what these connections and dependencies are ahead of time enables you to identify potential vulnerabilities and limitations earlier where it is less costly and impact-ful to address.

Establish Design Requirements

Requirements should be the basis of all design decisions, functional, security, compliance, or otherwise. Having a formal set of docu-mented requirements provides guidance and rationale for component creation.

Requirements should follow the SMART rule to ensure their qual-ity (Mannion & Keepence, 1995): Specific, Measurable, Attainable, Realizable, and Traceable.

Specific Requirements need to be clear and understandable with a sufficient level of detail to understand what is being asked of the system or component. A requirement defines exit criteria for system or component development, thus clear requirements are required to ensure that the system performs as expected.

Specific requirements are also simple, in that a single require-ment should describe a single function of the system or component. Complex requirements need to be broken down into multiple individ-ual requirements to enable testing. One trick to find complex require-ments is to look for use of the word "and". For example, "The system shall display the time and weather" should be broken down into two individual requirements.

Note that complex requirements may be acceptable in human pro-cesses where an individual's job description defines their roles and responsibilities. Using simple requirements for that approach may come off as micromanagement.

Measurable Requirements should describe an aspect of the system or component which can be tested or quantified in some way. In other words, we need to be able to prove that the system or compo-nent can meet the requirement. Business or organizational goals for the system should not be requirements because there is no way to validate whether the system or component can meet the goal prior to release.

Attainable   Requirements are the basis of defining acceptable criteria for release, and therefore it is important for all requirements to be attainable. While it would be great to have a service which has 100% availability or infinite logging, reality tells us that these requirements will never be met by any system. Instead, focus on realistic and attainable requirements such as 99.99% availability or 180 days of logging retained. If the service exceeds those thresholds and happens to provide 100% availability that's just a sign of good engineering work.

Realizable   Not every project is funded to deliver a highly available system with all the latest security technologies. Requirements levied on a system must be capable of realization given the budget and time provided. Many times, we must make sacrifices in design based on provided resources, and requirements should reflect resource availability.

Traceable   Adding requirements costs money and time; therefore, every requirement should be traceable back to their origin as an organizational need. This traceability ensures justification for the investment required to produce the capability designed by the requirement and helps provide sponsorship should costs, resources, or timeframes be affected by it.

For example, imagine you were developing a secure facility and one of the requirements included installation of pop-up barriers at all entrances. During project execution, it becomes apparent that there are a variety of unanticipated costs or delays associated with installing the barriers. Traceability enables the requirement to be linked to a sponsor and an organizational requirement. The sponsor may decide to add additional funding to the project or forego the barriers depending on other organizational factors. Without traceability, it would be impossible to justify the expenditure.

Define Use and Cryptography Standards

While cryptography is firmly rooted in the technology domain, the underlying essence (the need to a standardized baseline for data security) is universal. Establishing a baseline standard for data security ensures information will maintain a minimum level of protection at rest, in transit, and in use.

Establishing these standards is also typically associated with compliance requirements. For example, a contract with a partner may require special handling of their sensitive information, or the type of information (such as healthcare data) may be subject to regulation altogether.

Manage the Security Risk of Using Third-Party Components

Some level of risk occurs each time your system uses an external or third-party entity. That said, almost every system is likely to incorporate some third-party components or services. It is important to manage risk associated with use of these external or externally created entities when this occurs.

Managing risk goes back to our concepts of access and authorization. First, limit access by third-party components to only what is necessary for operation. This limitation ensures that a compromise of the component does not enable an attacker to spread to areas of the system which are unnecessary for the component to operate normally.

Second, always use least privilege design when granting authorization to any identity used by the component. Be critical of any requests for administrative authorization as they may be indicative of a poor security practices used in design or development.

Third, consider the implications of any external service being unavailable. An outage may directly impact your services operation if the third-party component is on the critical path for any availability sensitive information.

Finally, reduce risk to any confidentiality or integrity sensitive information by limiting the information provided to or processed by the third-party component to only what is necessary for its operation. When sensitive information must be processed by the component, ensure it is handled in accordance with organizational security standards in any contracts signed with the third-party organization.

Use Approved Tools

Information can only truly be protected when we trust the component and tools used within the system. For example, confidentiality may no longer be guaranteed if a user copies confidentiality sensitive information out of the system or one of the applications integrated with the system into an unapproved application. The unapproved application may not enforce the same security requirements designed within the system, thereby introducing risk.

From the technology perspective, this practice focuses on ensuring that only proper development tools are used to build the system and its components, and that the integrity of those tools is verified. Using unapproved tools may reduce reliability or induce vulnerabilities or backdoors due to flaws or integrity issues.

Perform Static Analysis Security Testing (SAST)

SAST refers to analysis of weaknesses based on how a component is designed. In technology, this refers to identifying flaws and logic errors in source code, such as overflows, injection attacks, or cross-site scripting. These flaws are cause vulnerabilities which can be used to establish illegitimate authorization within the system.

For other systems, this is essentially reviewing the design for weaknesses. For example, a static analysis security test of a lock design might involve ensuring that all aspects of the lock's design can withstand its rated durability, identifying any potential unintended way to open the lock without the key, or identifying backdoors. This review might help identify weaknesses before the lock design is finalized and mass produced, potentially avoiding making a bad name for the lock manufacturer.

Perform Dynamic Analysis Security Testing (DAST)

As its name might suggest, DAST involves providing test inputs to the system and its components to proactively identify flaws or vulnerabilities. This process is ideal for proactively identifying complex flaws which evade static analysis.

In technology, this is commonly performed using applications called fuzzers which provide specially crafted inputs designed to identify software flaws which may be abused by an attacker. For example, if a parameter is supposed to accept any value from 1 to 10 the fuzzer might supply it with 0, –1, 11, or "q" to see if the application is able to accommodate. Additionally, these applications will try values designed to exploit code injection flaws, such as supplying a single apostrophe to see if the application is vulnerable to SQL injection.

DAST is performed in the physical world when products undergo a certification process. For example, hurricane windows and doors are subject to a 2 × 4 board being launched at them at various points to determine whether the windows might fail during a storm. Many biometric security products are assessed on the basis of on their crossover error rate, which is a measurement of its accuracy in identifying fake authentication attempts compared to legitimate ones.

In the human process world, DAST is used when a restaurant has a preopening event where customers are used to test the staff's ability to handle customer orders at scale. Analysis of the number of resources and their roles may provide a good estimate of whether they will be able to handle the load, whereas flooding the restaurant with customers prior to opening enables the manager to validate it.

Perform Penetration Testing

Penetration testing enables third-party validation of a system's security. During penetration testing, a security professional attempts to find, exploit, and document flaws in the system – typically using any nondestructive means available.

Where possible, penetration tests should not be performed by individuals who were part of the security design or service development. Using an external team provides a fresh perspective and knowledge of different techniques. Additionally, professional penetration testers typically can replicate some of the latest attack techniques.

Penetration tests are not only for testing software. These processes are also effective at finding flaws in security devices or training needs within human processes. For example, many organizations use phishing services as a training tool for users. Security professionals may try to audit organizational security by finding ways to bypass checkpoints, search for wireless networks with weak credentials, or identify doors using weak authentication.

Establish a Standard Incident Response Process

Incidents happen and its critical to have a process for handling them when they do. Having an incident response plan helps to provide direction in times of crisis. That organized response is critical to reducing loss or downtime.

We will discuss incident response planning in our upcoming chapter called "Respond".

References

Bell. D. E., & LaPadula, L. J. (1973, November). *Secure Computer Systems: Mathematical Foundations.* Retrieved from Defense Technical Information Center: https://apps.dtic.mil/dtic/tr/fulltext/u2/770768.pdf

Haerder, T., & Reuter, A. (1983, December). *Principles of Transaction-Oriented Database Recovery.* Retrieved from The Association for Computing Machinery: https://dl.acm.org/doi/10.1145/289.291

Mannion, M., & Keepence, B. (1995, April). *SMART Requirements.* Retrieved from The Association for Computing Machinery: https://dl.acm.org/doi/pdf/10.1145/224155.224157

Mitre Corporation. (1975, June 30). *MTR-3153: Integrity Considerations for Secure Computer Systems.* Retrieved from UC Davis Computer Security Lab: http://seclab.cs.ucdavis.edu/projects/history/papers/biba75.pdf

9
DETECT

Something is wrong. Perhaps the system isn't acting as it should have been, some confidential data made it out to an external entity, or suddenly a bunch of data or services have been destroyed. Incidents happen all the time and it is important to take a measured approach to ensure you maximize impact without causing further damage or ruining forensic integrity.

The Security Uncertainty Principle

Heisenberg's famous uncertainty principle teaches us that the more we increase the precision at which we measure a particle's position the less precisely we can measure its momentum. In other words, we must sacrifice knowledge of its state to better gather data about its activity over time.

The same concept is true in security. Given less than infinite resources it is impossible to gather complete information about both a system's state and operation; therefore, we must make trade-offs. These trade-offs come in the form of focusing our monitoring on our most vulnerable or high value assets, while still maintaining the ability to perform static analysis throughout the system when necessary.

The goal of detection is to enable identification of security incidents in a cost-effective manner. To achieve this, we must identify the optimal balance between breadth, frequency, depth, retention, and cost. This balance ultimately defines the efficiency and effectiveness of our monitoring capability. In other words:

- We need enough breadth to cover the attack surfaces of the system
- We need a high enough monitoring frequency to ensure that we do not miss critical events

- We need sufficient depth to enable detection and response
- We need long enough retention to enable incident triage without executing a full forensic investigation each time
- We need to ensure that our detection strategy is cost-effective

A successful detection strategy should include monitoring of key operational activities paired with a periodic static analysis to provide depth. Monitoring is ideal for providing early warning, but we must not place all our trust in that bucket. Performing a periodic static analysis review of the system enables a deeper review and the opportunity to catch something we might not have noticed beforehand.

Types of Analysis

As we get into detection, response, and recovery, it is important to discuss the two different very types of analysis used in these processes: static and dynamic analysis. These capabilities complement each other well when used together to monitor or analyze the security of a system. That said, implementing only one or the other leaves a critical gap in an organization's ability to detect malicious activity.

Dynamic Analysis

Dynamic analysis techniques monitor a system and its components over time. These systems capture a running log of activity performed by the system and its components looking for trends or patterns which might indicate security concerns. These systems are the "security cameras" of detection and are what most organizations focus on for maintaining the day-to-day security of operations.

Time is typically the primary key of dynamic analysis; therefore, these systems tend to excel at comparing patterns of recent activity. In other words, dynamic analysis will be most helpful if you are looking to analyze the volume of events of a given type which happened on a system.

The drawback of a dynamic analysis system is that you are unlikely to have complete detail about each of these events. These systems typically reduce the amount of information captured at each event in favor of capturing a large volume of events, sort of how security cameras normally capture lower resolution or framerate images when compared to photographs.

Some examples of dynamic analysis include:

- Security cameras
- Intrusion detection systems
- Security guards or policemen
- Endpoint detection and response (EDR) systems
- User entity baseline analytics (UEBA) systems
- Antivirus on-access scanning capabilities
- Home security systems

Static Analysis

In a static analysis system, data are captured about the current state of a system and its components all at once. This approach enables a larger amount of information to be collected about relevant files and configurations, thus improving the ability to compare the state of the system. Using our previous analogy, these systems would be equivalent to high-resolution photographs.

By capturing the state of a system an analyst can perform a baseline comparison and identify deviations. Once a suspicious or malicious file or configuration is identified, static analysis enables the analyst to determine the prevalence of the condition based on information captured from elsewhere in the system.

Since static analysis focuses on the state of the system, timestamps collected are based on when files or configurations were created, last modified, or deleted. This is conducive to timelining and enables the analyst to review the history of the system beyond the recent past.

Static analysis has one major drawback – by itself, it provides little information about a system's operation. Luckily, this can pair well with dynamic analysis to provide a comprehensive view of the system's state and operation.

Common examples of static analysis tools include:

- Photographs
- Performing an on-demand antivirus scan
- Forensic disk capture software

- Vulnerability scanners
- Disassemblers, debuggers, and crash dump analysis applications
- Crime scene investigators or detectives

Types of Detection

Capturing information about a system's state and\or operation is just the start of the detection process. Once captured, we need to apply detection methodologies to surface indicators of suspicious or potentially malicious activity. This is typically accomplished through one of a variety of methods which use signature detection, anomaly detection, or machine learning.

Signature

Signature detection searches for patterns of potentially suspicious or known malicious activity. When written properly, these detections tend to be more reliable than anomaly detection techniques because they are based on a known pattern of attack.

Signatures are the most prevalent technique for detection because they are the simplest in concept. When an attack technique is identified, an analyst determines how they can uniquely and accurately identify it within the system. The signature is then deployed using the available detection technologies which monitor the system and its components through either static or dynamic analysis.

A signature detection doesn't always have to be 100% accurate. In fact, it is valuable to have tiers of signatures with different confidence levels attached. Signatures boasting perfect accuracy suffer from the need for the attack to have already been seen before. This means that these highly accurate signatures will likely never catch an attack if they use a new technique.

Low fidelity signatures can be valuable for detecting previously unknown techniques. This type of signature detection should reliably identify a techniques which appear suspicious but alone may not necessarily imply malice. These signatures are typically scored based on their individual accuracy and compared to a threshold to determine whether analysts should be alerted or action should be taken.

Most products that perform detection are fed by one or more threat intelligence sources. Threat intelligence provides information about patterns known to be used in attacks based on a broader dataset than is available to an individual customer. This type of service improves detection by supplying pre-built signatures based on attacks seen elsewhere to proactively detect and respond to known attacks.

Examples of signature-based detection are everywhere, including:

- Antivirus software
- Identifying suspicious purchase patterns in credit card fraud detection
- Wanted posters
- Threat intelligence feeds

Anomaly

Anomaly detection techniques enable identification of suspicious or malicious activity by comparing it to a baseline to detect abnormalities which may be indicative of an attack.

The benefit of anomaly detection is that you do not need a signature to detect a threat. This enables anomaly detection to pick up previously unseen attack techniques the first time they are used.

Unfortunately, this capability comes at a cost – anomaly detection is inherently noisy. An analyst will likely spend more time analyzing data to find malicious activity when compared to other methods. One of the big challenges of anomaly detection is the significant number of anomalies inherent to most system, referred to as the tail problem.

Anomaly detection begins by learning what normal looks like for the system and its components. It is important that the system is not compromised during this analysis, otherwise it may learn that the compromised state is normal.

Let's look a few different types of anomaly detection to gain a better understanding of this methodology.

Volume Over Time Measuring the volume of activity over time enables detection of sudden deviations. These fluctuations could be analyzed in comparison to how the system operates normally or relative to the volume of other similar components in the system. For example, a sudden increase in network traffic volume might indicate a denial-of-service attack or data exfiltration.

Low-Count Analysis Another detection capability involves finding low-count configurations or actions among components within the system. This approach is helpful in identifying outliers which may be indication of a backdoor. This technique can be used to detect anomalous configurations in static analysis or anomalous activities over time with dynamic analysis. Examples of backdoors which can be picked up using static analysis include:

- Identifying principals with no known legitimate use
- Finding undocumented authorization grants in an access control list
- Use of unauthorized components, such as an application which provides remote control
- A component communicating with an unknown destination

Key-Value Pair Analysis Key-value pair analysis identifies anomalies by identifying values which are commonly paired together, then searching for outliers in the otherwise consistent pattern.

For example, imagine we were comparing a list of truck drivers and their stops. We could probably find a trend that most drivers stop at some gas stations and restaurants on their way to their destinations. If this pattern is highly consistent, we may be able to identify suspicious behavior by analyzing stops at other locations along the way. These stops could include attempts to sell product illegitimately or could just as easily be visits to family or friends.

Another example occurs when a user always logs on to the same computer every day. In this case, the key would be the user account and the computer would be the value. If suddenly the user begins logging on to a large number of machines which are not normal for them it might represent malicious activity.

Chronological Anomaly Analysis   Sometimes you know that a given event or component within the system always happens at a specific time. Deviations from that normal pattern would be an anomaly which might be worth investigating. This type of pattern might indicate that something is wrong within the system or that a component of the system may be compromised. These are chronological anomalies.

For example, users typically log on and work the same hours each day and the same days each week. If suddenly one of your users begins logging on in the middle of the night or during their weekend this could mean that their credentials may have been stolen.

Another example comes from analyzing the length of time a task takes to complete. If a security guard's rounds normally take 30 minutes and suddenly take over an hour this might indicate that something may have gone wrong.

Geographic Distance Analysis   Sometimes you can use geolocation to identify patterns of suspicious behavior. This technique is particularly useful in locating anomalous logon locations. For example, if a user lives in Europe and always logs on from the same location, then suddenly logs on from a different country, either the user is on vacation or their account may be compromised.

Machine Learning

Machine learning provides somewhat of a balance of the previous two types of detection. This technique can detect previously unknown threats without needing to first create the signature. It also provides a detection rate which is typically higher than anomaly detection if implemented properly.

In machine learning detection, a set of files, configurations, or activities are fed into an algorithm and deemed malicious or benign. This process repeats until the algorithm efficiently identifies previously unknown malicious activity and detects few, if any, clean activities as malicious.

Like anomaly detection, machine learning is best trained on a relatively clean dataset. While malicious activities can be identified and trained out of the dataset, subtle aspects of malicious activity may be inadvertently trained into the dataset due to the compromised aspects tainting otherwise clean data.

One of the challenges that may be associated with machine learning is the need for a large volume of data. Effectively training an algorithm can take thousands to millions of datapoints to ensure accuracy, which may pose a challenge for smaller operations.

The other possible issue with machine learning detection is what I like to call the "42 problem". With any machine learning system, you end up finding the answer to your question without really knowing how you got there. In other words, there is not really a way to dig into the algorithm to determine *why* something is malicious. You instead need to trust the algorithm's decision-making process and history of detection accuracy somewhat blindly.

Signal-to-Noise Ratio

Many detection techniques are not perfect. Even a well-written signature detection has the potential for inadvertently detecting something benign as malicious (known as a false-positive) or missing something malicious (known as a false-negative) on occasion.

The signal-to-noise ratio of a detection technique is a measurement of how accurately it detects malicious activity as a ratio of its accidental detection of benign activity as malicious. This acts as a measurement of effectiveness and quantifies the level of trust you can place in determinations made by that capability.

The signal-to-noise ratio of your detection capability directly translates to its effectiveness. A system with too many false-positive detections will typically be ignored, whereas one with too many false negatives won't provide any value. The goal in detection is to find the sweet spot where the value of the signal outweighs the impact of its noise.

Detection Confidence Levels

One way to improve the efficacy of detection is to include confidence scores associated with each detection. Using multiple "noisy" detections paired with confidence scores that reflect the accuracy of the detection improves the effectiveness of otherwise noisy detections. In these systems, thresholds are established on the basis of the sums of individual detection efficacy scores to determine whether this is something upon which action should be taken.

Most systems will also implement a variety of severity levels for detections based on a combination of the overall detection confidence score and the severity of the activity detected. Severity levels help analysts prioritize their investigation to focus on the most pressing security concerns of the organization first.

Tuning for Suppression or Amplification

Another approach to improving the detection involves tuning the detection capability. Sometimes false-positives will happen regardless of how confidence levels are implemented. Other times, you might have a specific condition in which the system should be more paranoid, such as if a detection should appear within your authentication system. To accommodate these cases, it is important to enable the detection system to be tunable for both suppression and amplification.

Suppression tuning involves configuring the system to explicitly ignore a specific detection in a specific condition. For example, a legitimate software package may cause detections under normal operation. To avoid unnecessary work due to false-positive detections it is important to suppress known benign detections. Suppression should be performed on as narrow of a scope as possible to ensure that detections of other potentially suspicious activity still fire.

Amplification tuning is essentially changing the threshold at which detections cause an alert or increasing alert severity based on some attribute of the detection. For example, alerts on accounts with widespread administrative authority warrant a higher severity than those with normal user authorization. Just the same, alerts occurring on systems which handle sensitive information or perform authentication should be handled with higher priority than other systems.

Improving Signal-to-Noise Ratio by System Design

Another way to improve signal-to-noise ratio is in the design of the system itself. Detections work by identifying abnormal activity within the system. This means that we can improve the effectiveness of detection by improving consistency of the system's operation.

Standardization

Standardization is the first approach to improving detection. Anomaly detection works best if every portion of the system looks the same from a configuration and operation perspective. From a software perspective, this usually means ensuring every instance of a component looks the exact same as others performing the same role. Through standardization anomalies become more anomalous, therefore allowing lower thresholds for detection and increasing the efficiency and effectiveness of the system overall.

Simplification

Simplification is another way to improve the effectiveness of detection. Anomalies become more difficult to detect as you increase the number of different actions a component performs.

Imagine a factory where each machine has a very well-defined role in the manufacturing process. It would be immediately apparent if one of the machines in the system suddenly began acting erratically. Now compare that machine to a personal laptop computer where the action of the component is entirely up to the user. In our first case, the component performs highly repetitive tasks more like a machine, whereas the laptop works more like a tool. Identifying anomalies in the machine is significantly easier than trying to find them based on usage of a tool.

The D.I.E. Triad

Security professionals Kelly Shortridge and Nicole Forsgren proposed a new approach to integrating DevOps and Security at Black Hat 2019 (Shortridge & Forsgren, 2019). In their presentation, they proposed a new model for DevOps design which sought to improve the security and reliability of software systems by design.

Their presentation recommended three design concepts that should be followed to ensure ongoing security and reliability of a system:

- Distributed – Use multiple instances of components or systems to support the same overarching goal
- Immutable – Components within the system should not change after they are deployed
- Ephemeral – Components within the system should have a very short lifespan

As we discussed in the previous chapter, distributed systems lead directly to improved availability. This ensures the system isn't bound by scale limitations and can scale automatically to meet demand.

The immutable aspect of a software system leads to highly standardized components which simplify detection. Any variance in a component within the system should be easily detectable by following the attributes of simplicity and standardization.

The last aspect, ephemerality, leads to improved detection and response capabilities by reducing the value of persistence. If we value components within our systems in the same way as we value credentials, the length of time a component exists directly translates to its value to an attacker. In addition, if the individual components are immutable it implies that we can destroy and regenerate a compromised component to reestablish system integrity. To achieve this, we must ensure each component has recoverability.

Using Edges to Improve Detection

The level of consistency of a system directly translates to its security and the ability to detect malicious activity. Therefore, try to segment highly consistent components from inconsistent ones using an edge where possible. Narrowing the scope of components within an edge creates a more highly consistent system and forces other components and systems to communicate over intended means of access. This concept goes back to our discussion on monolithic versus microservice architecture and the overall benefit of simplicity in design.

What to Monitor

A system provides almost limitless aspects that can be monitored, though many provide little value compared to their overhead cost. Monitoring every aspect of a component within a system increases the likelihood that information required for forensics is available, but often this becomes a pile of unanalyzed data that is paid for and left for expiration.

Access Across an Edge

Anytime access traverses an edge we should record the activity. Access across an edge means that communication is traversing areas of differing trust, which provides opportunity for tamper.

Access monitoring should include all inbound and outbound access across the edge. Inbound monitoring provides an opportunity to identify attack attempts from less or differently trusted sources. Monitoring outbound connections enables identification of potential theft or covert control channels.

Edge access monitoring has two generic categories: monitoring flow and content inspection. Systems which monitor flow are designed for high throughput, passively watching and logging traffic traversing an area. This approach trades context for performance and may be suitable for access points requiring high traffic volumes or when cost is a significant factor compared to security needs. Examples of this type of monitoring include security cameras and netflow logging.

Content inspection systems intercept and inspect access attempts to proactively identify suspicious activity. Content inspection costs overhead and reduces throughput but provides increased confidence in security as a result. Examples of content inspection systems include

- Physical security checkpoints
- Proxy servers with SSL interception
- Reverse proxy
- Email gateways

Access monitoring should include comprehensive coverage of all access points which traverse the edge to be effective. Lack of comprehensive access monitoring provides the opportunity for covert communication, thereby reducing the value of the monitoring capability overall.

Authentication

Identity is one of the most important aspects when designing security for an authorization control system, making authentication one of the most important aspects for monitoring. Adverse activity can be quickly identified when authentication activity is trended based on location, time of day, day of week, identity to system key-value pair association, and when compared to attack signatures.

Authentication should be logged each time a credential is validated (success and failure), including when credential validation is deferred across a trust. During incident response, authentication logs help an analyst or incident responder identify which systems and components might require deeper analysis in search of potentially suspicious activity.

Authentication information should include the following attributes (where available) at a minimum:

- The source location where the authentication occurred
- The system or component where authentication was processed
- The domain that the credential was issued from
- The method used for authentication
- Any pertinent information required to chain together proxying of access or authentication

Some examples of authentication to monitor include when:

- Individuals authenticate to the security guard to obtain a visitor badge
- Users are authenticated to an authentication system
- Physical keys are issued to employees
- A passport is reviewed to grant a traveler access to a country
- A user establishes any sort of session to a service
- Anytime credential translation occurs

Authorization

Anytime authorization occurs there is a potential for forensic value, thus we should try to record any authorization requested by a principal to help build a timeline of activities during incident response. That said, logging every authorization request may not be feasible in every system due to cost or performance. This section highlights the most important authorization for monitoring and forensics.

Administrative authorization should be logged anytime it is requested, regardless of whether it was granted. This type of authorization runs the risk of compromising either system integrity or credential confidentiality, thereby enabling an attacker to elevate their authorization or maintain persistent control over the system or one of its components.

Any authorization request to sensitive information should be logged, regardless of result. Authorization requests to sensitive information help the organization understand what may have been compromised during the attack and may provide insight into their interests.

Authorization requests to principals and groups which provide either administrative authorization or authorization to sensitive information are another important aspect of detection. Attempts to discover or change these entities may indicate an attacker attempting to profile the system's security to identify high value principals or attempts to add principals to a sensitive group.

Finally, any authorization requests to the authentication components of the system should be monitored to ensure ongoing integrity. This includes creation, deletion, or modification of any principals, groups, trusts, domains, or securables (access control lists). Attempted changes to these components provide significant value when determining the scope of a compromise.

Translation and Detection

Access, credential, or principal translation can pose challenges in correlating attacker activity because it exchanges the actual identity or method of access used by the attacker with a different one. If you're not careful, this can significantly weaken anomaly detection or correlation and result in missed detections.

For example, let's say a spy checks in to the front desk using their ID and is issued a visitor badge with door access. The spy enters a few rooms, steals some sensitive information, and tampers with important documents. This activity can be easily correlated to the visitor badge which enables you to determine where the spy went while they were inside; however, to correlate it back to the individual you would need a log entry with the identity they presented paired with the visitor badge they were issued.

Whenever translation occurs it is crucial to log the original untranslated attribute and the new translated attribute including any information that may be helpful in associating translated activity with its original untranslated counterpart. By doing this, you enable humans and systems to perform correlation based on the original untranslated attribute and thereby increase the likelihood of detection.

Exceptions, Faults, and Failures

Many times, when an attacker attempts to exploit a vulnerability within a system or component it causes abnormal activity or deviations from its normal operation. Monitoring for and investigating these deviations can enable early detection of attempts to exploit or abuse the system.

Where possible, log and monitor any failures or deviations from normal operation to provide early detection of suspicious activity.

Reference

Shortridge, K., & Forsgren, N. (2019, August 7). *Controlled Chaos: The Inevitable Marriage of Devops and Security*. Retrieved from Black Hat: https://i.blackhat.com/USA-19/Wednesday/us-19-Shortridge-Controlled-Chaos-The-Inevitable-Marriage-Of-DevOps-And-Security.pdf

10
Respond

So you got pwned. Your detection processes worked and suddenly you have found unexplained activity within your system – and that activity appears to be an attacker. This chapter will walk you through the process of characterizing, scoping, and investigating attacker activity with the goal of eviction and recovery.

Knowing how to hunt is perhaps the most valuable, yet least documented, asset to any incident responder. Skilled incident responders seem to innately know where to look for the next piece of information but have historically lacked (at least to my knowledge) a general model that can be used to tie all of this together.

Targeting

At the most basic level an attack can be categorized based on its level of targeting. Targeting is the amount of focus an attacker places on compromising a specific target versus executing a broad attack campaign designed to compromise anyone susceptible to the attack technique.

Every attack has some level of targeting. Even broadly targeted attacks rely on some predictable aspect of their target, such as their language, a product or service they use, or a location where the attack takes place. In contrast, highly targeted operations might focus on compromising a single organization, individual, or component.

Let's take a look at some of the differences between broadly and narrowly targeted attacks:

Table 10.1

ATTRIBUTE	BROADLY TARGETED ATTACK	NARROWLY TARGETED ATTACK
Focus	Targets a broad audience	Targets a specific individual or organization
Customization	Low degree of customization to target	High degree of customization to target
Process	Highly repeatable, automated	Custom strategy which evolves based on feedback
Recovery	Simply remove the threat	Response requires coordinated strike

As an example, imagine comparing a strategy used to scam people out of money to one designed to steal a specific piece of intelligence held by an organization. The money scam attack will likely focus effort on anyone who seems susceptible and likely has money, whereas the intelligence collection can only truly be gathered from a very specific organization.

This difference changes the way in which we respond to the attack. Less targeted attacks are unlikely to have a high level of coordination. Therefore, many times this type of attack can be simply contained and removed without much thought – we can simply call the police to get rid of the scammer.

Highly targeted attacks are typically more sophisticated and coordinated. Simply addressing attacks as they arise is less likely to be effective when dealing with a determined and coordinated attacker. In fact, by immediately responding to activity as you detect it you inform the attacker that you are aware of their presence. This is likely to cause them to reassess and change their strategy to dodge your detection.

The Phases of an Attack

Human-operated attacks can be broken down into phases based on techniques employed by the attacker. In cybersecurity, these techniques have been broken down by a number of different organizations each with their own variations. The most common theme among them involves five major phases:

1. Reconnaissance: The attacker surveils the target to identify vulnerabilities and susceptibilities that can be exploited to provide access and authorization.
2. Initial entry and persistence: The attacker exploits a weakness and establishes a durable foothold within the target system using some form of persistence mechanism.
3. Lateral traversal: The attacker uses their persistence point to pivot between different components within the system in search of the access and authorization they require to carry out their attack (assuming the attacker hasn't attained the necessary authorization during the initial breach).

4. Privilege escalation: The attacker establishes access and authorization necessary to perform their intended attack, through either exploitation or credential theft.

5. Impact: The attacker uses their authorization to carry out their intended attack.

Recently, the industry standardized on a new framework developed by Mitre (the same organization which manages the National Vulnerability Database). Mitre ATT&CK (which stands for Adversarial Tactics, Techniques, and Common Knowledge) organizes activities performed during a cyberattack into 14 different tactics. Each of these tactics then contains numerous techniques, which are specific implementations of the tactic.

The ATT&CK framework is used in a variety of ways:

- It helps define and rationalize activities performed during a cyberattack
- It serves as a framework for testing the detective capabilities of security products
- It is used to measure training and staff readiness
- It provides a means to structure and compare threat intelligence
- It helps identify gaps in detection design

To help understand the phases of an attack we will analyze plot points for the 2001 movie Oceans 11 for their alignment. If you haven't seen this movie yet I would highly recommend watching it now because there are spoilers ahead (and because it's a great movie). It is also helpful to understand the context of the scenes to understand their alignment.

Let's take a look into the different tactics covered by the ATT&CK framework.

Reconnaissance

Reconnaissance is a tactic used by an attacker to discover available forms of access, authorization checks, exploitable vulnerabilities, and opportunities for credential theft prior to initial access. Attackers will typically build a profile on individuals, systems, weaknesses, patterns of activity, and other valuable intelligence to identify optimal patterns of attack and ways to increase the likelihood of their success.

Reconnaissance can occur actively or passively. Common techniques involved during the reconnaissance phase include:

- Photographing individuals, access points, authorization checks, or weaknesses
- Monitoring conversations in locations where employees might gather to talk about work
- Scanning available systems or components over a network to determine available forms of access
- Researching key individuals from the organization to build a social engineering profile or identify people in roles that might have access to sensitive information
- Searching for organizational credentials on password leak websites
- Determining business partners to help identify possible entry points where security might be lax
- Scanning for available vulnerabilities

The first example of reconnaissance in Oceans 11 is when Danny Ocean obtains a copy of the floor plan for the Bellagio vault through a connection. This floor plan is key for the heist team to determine their plan of attack since it details many of the defenses they are going to need to defeat in their mission to steal the money.

Another example of reconnaissance in Oceans 11 is when Linus shadows Terry Benedict to figure out his normal routine. By shadowing, Linus learns of any opportunities the team might have to intercept his vault codes.

Resource Development

Resource development is all about creating or obtaining any capability required for an attack against the victim. These might be software exploits, backdoors, hardware, infrastructure, partnerships, hiring team members, or any other acquisition tied to the attack. Some examples might include:

- Creating fake ID cards or other credentials to bypass authentication

- Developing exploits or malware for use in the attack
- Building or acquiring any hardware required to carry out the attack
- Purchasing or renting domains, botnets, credentials, or cloud resources for use in the attack

There are a number of examples of resource development performed in Oceans 11. First the team needed money, so they reached out to Reuben because they shared a common enemy (Terry Benedict). This susceptibility led Reuben to fund the operation in a condition when he otherwise likely wouldn't have, so technically Danny Ocean may have exploited Ruben's susceptibility a bit in the process as well.

Another great example of resource development occurred when the team built a working replica of the Bellagio vault. Without this replica there would be no way for the heist to have worked, and there was no realistic way they could have pulled off the heist otherwise.

Other examples of resource development include:

- Hiring the heist team members
- Buying vans
- Acquiring the Bellagio waiter and casino floor worker outfits
- Buying the suit for Saul to impersonate an international arms dealer
- Acquiring the pinch from the California Institute of Advanced Sciences

Initial Access

Initial access is when the actual attack portion begins from the target's perspective. The attacker executes their plan using tools they built in the resource development phase. If successful, the attacker will gain a foothold within the victim system.

Initial access could occur using a variety of techniques including:

- A phishing attack
- Seeding USB drives with malware and placing them around the target's office building
- Compromising a business partner who has access to information systems at the target

- Using one of the organization's public-facing services to compromise the server or monitor email communication
- Using social engineering to reset a credential

There were multiple examples of initial access performed in Oceans 11. One example happens when the Malloy brothers, disguised as casino floor workers, start fighting over not having an ID card to get into the back room while pushing the cash cart (with Yen inside). This scene intentionally occurs right in front of another casino floor worker who agrees to take the cash cart to the vault to prevent them from making a scene.

Another example occurs when Linus, disguised as a Nevada Gaming Commission member, incriminates Frank Catton as a felon. This causes Terry Benedict to bring them behind the badge access door for interrogation.

Other examples of initial access include Linus portraying a doctor and the Malloy brothers pretending to be emergency medical technicians to take care of Saul, or when the heist team pretended to be SWAT team members to gain access to the vault.

Execution

Execution is any action performed by the attacker, which results in the compromised system or component performing illegitimate activity on their behalf. The ATT&CK framework categorizes this behavior based on the means of execution rather than by the activity being performed.

Examples might include:

- Running scripts on a compromised endpoint
- Performing actions by running commands using a discovered SQL injection vulnerability
- Tricking a victim into disclosing sensitive information after social engineering
- Performing actions using a hijacked wireless device

Execution is a rather generic category that can technically be applied to just about any action which occurs in the compromised system post-breach. Additionally, the association with execution frameworks (i.e., scripting engines, application programming interfaces) makes it difficult to associate with activities outside of the software world. It would be like describing activity as verbal, physical, or any other attribute underlying how an action is carried out.

Technically any activity performed by the Oceans 11 crew after the breach could be classified as execution. Additionally, since this is a movie there are fewer unnecessary actions performed by the crew in an effort to discover their environment. The only purely execution action would likely be when Basher plans to tamper with the power grid, but instead learns that the power company identified the weakness. This would also have occurred external to the casino (by attacking an external dependency – the power grid) thus it is a bit of a stretch.

Persistence

Persistence occurs whenever an attacker tampers with a system or component to provide a form of durable access, authorization, or authentication. Persistence acts as insurance for the attacker ensuring their ability to maintain control over the compromised entity in the event of a response action.

There are a wide variety of types of persistence. Literally anything which can provide covert dedicated access, authorization, or authentication can be used as a form of persistence. From an ATT&CK perspective, persistence is the execution of an action by an attacker to establish this illegitimate capability within the system or component. For example, an attacker might:

- Create a user account for their own dedicated use to prevent broad credential changes
- Modify an access control list to intentionally grant excessive authorization to otherwise unprivileged principals
- Install backdoor software such as a reverse shell, webshell, or remote administration tool
- Disable a lock or other authorization control to enable illegitimate access
- Implant a spy at the target organization to perform actions on their behalf
- Install a wiretap or retroreflector to listen in on otherwise secure communication

In Oceans 11, there were a number of times where persistence was established:

- Oscar, the insider security guard who allows Danny Ocean to gain access to the Bellagio floor plan
- When Linus used a stolen ID card to gain access to the server room and install wiretaps on the surveillance system
- Frank Catton became an insider when he transferred to the Bellagio with illicit intentions
- The moment when Yen was pushed into the Bellagio vault in a cash cart he became a human form of persistence
- When Bulldog, the Bruiser is brought in to beat up Danny Ocean, which we later find out is a paid friend of Danny Ocean

Privilege Escalation

A privilege escalation occurs when an attacker tricks a higher privileged component to perform actions that would require authorization the attacker does not currently have on their behalf. In other words, the system has to lack some form of check to enable this condition to manifest. This is essentially an exploitation technique which enables an unprivileged attacker to perform privileged activities without requiring credential theft.

Some examples of privilege escalation include:

- Elevation of privilege exploits
- Social engineering whereby the victim makes a change on the attacker's behalf
- Injection attacks which allow the attacker to run arbitrary code under a system identity
- Tampering with an existing capability running in an administrative context to have it perform activities on your behalf

There are two main examples of privilege escalation used in Oceans 11. The first occurs when the Malloy brothers make a scene while dressed as Bellagio employees. The actual Bellagio employee tries to diffuse the situation by helping them out and pushing the cash cart (containing Yen) to the vault. The failures on the Bellagio employee's part that enable this is lack of proper authentication, susceptibility to a stressful situation, and not checking the integrity of the contents of the cash cart.

Our second privilege escalation occurs when Linus "forgets his pager" and tricks Terry Benedict into letting him escort himself out. In this case, Linus uses Terry's legitimate authority to get him past the door and abuses his misplaced trust leaving him granted with access to an otherwise secured area.

Defense Evasion

Defense evasion is all about avoiding detection. These activities include a variety of tactics used to avoid detection by either humans or software technologies. Some examples of this activity include:

- Disabling antimalware or EDR software
- Disabling or destroying security cameras
- Using uniforms to reduce suspicion
- Use of a rootkit to hide the presence of a malware implant
- Cutting communication lines to prevent an alarm system or guard from calling the authorities
- Use of a fake ID card or identity

Oceans 11 is full of examples of defense evasion. For example:

- The Malloy brothers use balloons to cover a security camera while Livingston Dell uses a stolen ID card to gain access to the server room
- Multiple times the heist crew used a fake video feed to override the actual video
- Using the pinch to shut off electricity and cause chaos throughout the casino
- When Danny Ocean and Linus used knock out gas and zip ties to tie up the guards

Credential Access

Activities in the credential access category include anything where an attacker obtains a credential for use in the attack. These techniques enable the attacker to either maintain existing or establish new authenticated sessions as the principal associated with the credential. This results in the attacker being able to perform any and all actions that the principal would be allowed over any form of access which accepts the credential.

Some examples of credential access include:

- Pass the hash, pass the ticket, and other enterprise single sign-on credential attacks
- Stealing an ID badge from an employee
- Searching through an email account for the word "password"
- Searching for email accounts belonging to the target organization in a password dump
- Using phishing to trick legitimate users into exposing their password

Oceans 11 has two notable examples of credential access. The first occurs when the dancer seduces the security guard, stealing his ID card in the process. The second example is when Linus is accusing Frank Catton of being a felon in front of Terry Benedict. When Frank lunges at him, Linus uses his pickpocket skills to lift the vault codes from Terry Benedict's pocket.

Discovery

Discovery is any post-breach reconnaissance activities performed by the attacker to learn about previously obscured aspects of the system. One might argue that there are a lot of similarities between reconnaissance and discovery – and you'd be right. The only major differences between reconnaissance and discovery pertain to the timeframe and available means of access. Technically, if the system exposed these services publicly this might all be classified as reconnaissance – but in today's state of technology that could pose significant risk.

Examples of discovery activities might include:

- Gaining information about the operating environment after exploitation
- Discovering privileged groups and accounts
- A bank robber identifying threats and key assets after they stick up a bank

In a real-world attack, the attacker is unlikely to know everything about their target's security posture prior to breach; however, in Oceans 11 their knowledge was fairly complete. The closest thing to discovery activity which occurred in the movie would probably be when they gained access to the camera system. For this to be discovery, though, they would need to have used it to learn about the security of the casino rather than simply surveilling.

Lateral Movement

Lateral movement occurs when an attacker moves around the system using credentials they've already obtained. The tactic is termed lateral movement because the attacker moves between components of equal value using legitimate access and authorization in search of higher value targets, such as credentials with broad administrative authorization.

Some examples of lateral movement include:

- Using a stolen ID card on random doors in search of anything of value
- Using stolen credentials to connect to other components within the system in search of higher powered credentials
- Use of an eDiscovery capability to search e-mail boxes for credentials or other valuable information
- Using a stolen passphrase or other identifying information to socially engineer other people into performing actions on your behalf

Lateral movement in the physical or human process world is a bit harder to define than in the technology space because authentication is not typically as formal of a process. In Oceans 11, the heist team used a variety of uniforms they acquired to masquerade as legitimate employees of the Bellagio casino. Uniforms are acceptable as a form of identity in many human processes; thus the team effectively used their outfits as a means of blending in and establishing illegitimate identity.

Another example of lateral traversal which led to persistence was when Linus used the stolen ID card to access the wire closet. In this situation he used a stolen ID card to gain access to a space where the actual owner of the ID card had the ability to enter.

Collection

Collection occurs when the attacker gathers (presumably confidentiality sensitive) information for exfiltration. This may include capturing information from available interfaces, such as cameras or microphones, or packaging existing information for later exfiltration. Examples of collection include:

- Using an archive utility to zip files for exfiltration
- Using an eDiscovery tool to search the victim's systems for keywords of interest
- Capturing video and/or audio feeds using a microphone or camera
- Placing sensitive files into a briefcase or suitcase

The most notable example of collection in Oceans 11 was when they made it into the casino vault and (presumably) started putting the money into the black duffel bags. This made exfiltration of the cash much simpler and covert.

The other example is technically whenever they tapped into the security cameras to monitor the team's activities and help them improve timing and dodge potential threats.

Command and Control

Command and control is any means of controlling any asset within the system using a communication channel.

Command and control is perhaps the most important asset to the attacker – it is what enables external operators to communicate with and control any of the compromised entities within the environment. For this reason, command and control channels are typically one of the most protected aspects of the attack.

Examples of command and control include:

- An attacker-controlled server hosted on the Internet
- A secret email account, DNS domain, or website used for communication
- Headsets, walkie-talkies, or other radio frequency communication

- A dead drop or dead letter box
- Steganography

In Oceans 11, the heist team performed command and control using earpieces and cell phones. While not sophisticated, these techniques were able to dodge timely detection by the victim enabling them to carry out their mission before the communication channel had been detected.

To show how important command and control is, consider how different the movie would have been had the two security guards from the casino checked Danny Ocean for an earpiece when they caught him. The victim would have been able to listen in on every command made and may have been able to identify the source broadcasting the communications to the team. Movie over.

Exfiltration

Exfiltration occurs when the attacker steals any collected information from the victim's system. This can be as simple as a single web post to a public server or as complicated as a prison break or VIP extraction. The attacker's goal during exfiltration is to get confidentiality sensitive information outside of the protection of the system for their use.

Examples of exfiltration include:

- Using an email forwarding rule to automatically send sensitive information to an attacker's email address
- Uploading stolen information to a website
- Reading a confidentiality sensitive document over a phone call or walkie-talkie
- Broadcasting sensitive information over a public medium

There was one obvious form of exfiltration in Oceans 11 – when the heist team walks out of the casino dressed as SWAT team members with duffel bags full of cash.

Impact

Finally, our last tactic is impact. Impact is the goal for attackers who want to hinder their target's operations. Whereas exfiltration is an attack against information confidentiality, impact typically targets integrity or availability.

Impact can be noticeable or covert. For example, a targeted ransomware or defacement attack makes it very clear that the attacker has control over a system (this is one of the intended reactions from the attack). On the other hand, the Stuxnet attack against Iranian nuclear refinement facilities subtly tampered with the system while secretly destroying the uranium.

Examples of impact include:

- Bombing a target
- Deploying a ransomware or system wiper application
- Defacing a website
- A labor union going on strike
- A distributed denial of service attack

Oceans 11 has one major example of impact – when the heist team streams the video of Terry Benedict choosing money over his girl-friend (Danny Ocean's ex-wife). This ultimately impacts Tess's availability, though one might also argue that it might be exfiltration. I'll let you be the judge of that.

Performing a Coordinated Response

A coordinated response to an attack is thought-out and executed in a very concerted manner, respecting the attacker's intellect and ensuring maximum impact. Taking a coordinated response means you shift your focus from removing the symptom of the attack to removing the attacker.

One challenge commonly faced in performing a coordinated response is an organization's bias for action. A coordinated response can take time and requires the organization to withhold reaction in exchange for a more comprehensive eviction. That said, time is of the essence in any targeted attack as the longer an attacker remains resident within the system the greater damage they can perform.

Many organizations focus on immediately responding to any malicious activity by eliminating the entity which caused the alert. This reaction can cause more harm than good by informing the attacker that you are aware of their presence. Once an attacker changes tactics you run the risk of no longer being able to track their activity, whereas the attacker likely still maintains durable control of the system.

In much of the world this reaction is called "whack-a-mole", named after the kids' game where a mole pops out of a hole and you whack it with a mallet (interesting aside, in South Korea this is referred to as ping pong, referring to the constant back-and-forth activity as you find new malicious activity). The likely result from this is that the attacker goes silent and maintains control without providing any cues as to how they are doing so.

Operational Security (OPSEC)

Operational security, or OPSEC, refers to protection of information pertaining to a sensitive activity. During response, this means ensuring that your adversary remains unaware of what you know about their footholds within a system and ensuring they remain unaware of any eviction plans.

The minimum level of OPSEC used during response and recovery is derived from a combination of the perceived attacker's skill and the depth and scope of the compromise. This becomes a challenge during response because typically you are not aware of either of these attributes. As such, the best plan is to establish a completely isolated infrastructure for communications that shares no relationship with the compromised system.

Another challenge occurs when the compromised system is associated with devices or individuals which are part of day-to-day operations. The capability of an attacker is determined by the sum of all authorization granted to any principal they control and the capability of any device controlled by the attacker. This means:

- If an attacker can authenticate as a user, they may be able to read any of their communications.
- If an attacker has or can compromise a device, they may be able to use its microphone, camera, or read files from its storage.

- If the attacker has an individual embedded within the organization (referred to as an insider threat), that individual may be able to inform the attacker of your plans or influence the investigation.
- If the attacker compromises a domain, any credentials authenticated by the domain become untrustworthy and securables controlled by the domain may be compromised.

For this reason, the best plan is to keep investigations small and compartmentalized. Where possible, follow these guidelines to help protect OPSEC during response and recovery:

- Involve only trustworthy individuals who have undergone a periodic background check.
- Consider establishing a new, and completely separate, communication infrastructure for each investigation.
- Always use strong credentials which have no security association with any potentially compromised system or component for investigation.
- Avoid communicating any details of an investigation outside of the trusted communication infrastructure.
- Consider enforcing encryption at rest on any artifacts of the investigation. The domain that manages credentials for protected artifacts should also have no association with any potentially compromised system or component.

Another very important, and often overlooked, aspect of OPSEC is time. Remember that ephemerality is one of the components of a strong security design, and the longer a given system exists, the more likely it is to be compromised. The longer an investigation and response take the more likely it is for sensitive details of the investigation to become compromised. For this reason, investigation and response should be as short-lived as possible, ideally measured in days or weeks – *not* months.

The ABCs of Incident Response

Every element of an incident can be broken down into four elements: the authentication used by the attacker to perform the action, the backdoor (means of access) used to perform the action, the communication path between the attacker and the backdoor, and any data which was stolen, tampered with, or destroyed as a result.

The ABCs also represent the assets controlled by the attacker which give them power within the system, identifying credentials which must be reset, forms of persistence to eliminate, and communication channels to block and monitor during eviction. These aspects of the breach focus on the human component of the attack rather than the impact and are the only true way to evict an embedded human adversary.

Authentication

Authentication refers to the identity aspect of the system or breach. Remember that authorization can only be derived from one of two places: exploitation or authentication. Exploitation is not always easy or reliable. The vulnerability that got an attacker into a system may not work on the next phase of attack unless the vulnerability is widespread, reliable, and common. This means that the attacker's best option in most cases is authentication.

Establishing authentication requires the attacker to perform one of the following attacks:

- Exploit credential weaknesses
- Capitalize on credential exposure
- Compromise an existing session running under an already established principal identity
- Tamper with the integrity of a domain
- Add a principal to a domain
- Add or modify credentials for a principal already in existence

Once compromised, this grants the attacker the ability to masquerade as the newly compromised identity to any service which will accept the credential. The value of this credential can be measured using the algorithm from our chapter on authentication:

$$Credential\ Value = \left(\sum_{Service} Authorization \right) \times Validity\ Period$$

Let's look at some of the different categories of authentication and how they pertain to a compromise.

Actual Identity Our first case is the most straightforward – the actual identity of the attacker. Most sophisticated attackers will try to conceal their actual identity if possible, sometimes creating an entirely fake persona and other times solely using compromised or fabricated identities.

The actual identity of an attacker is typically well hidden but may be exposed from time to time due to mistakes. For example:

- The attacker may connect to a system in a way which causes their computer to automatically try to authenticate them.
- An attacker may make a mistake and expose something real about their identity during conversation or expose subtle details about themselves through their accent or manner of speaking.
- The fake ID card created by the attacker may have a certain attribute which causes it to stand out.

These attributes of the real identity of the attacker can be used to covertly identify additional attacker activity, which may in turn identify other compromised accounts, backdoors, communication channels, or data.

Stolen Credentials Our second category of authentication is stolen credentials. This occurs when an attacker obtains a reusable credential for a principal within the system. Tracking an attacker who is using stolen credentials requires the hunter to differentiate what is normal versus what is abnormal for a given user principal.

Stolen credentials typically involve credential exposure or an authentication-based attack. This typically means that the credential is weak or has been exposed to a system or component whose integrity was compromised. This point of exposure may not always be identifiable by the analyst, but a best effort attempt should be made to determine this point.

One thing to be aware of when tracking suspicious use of credentials is insider threat. It is possible that the identity being abused is the attacker's real identity, thus it is best to avoid directly contacting the true owner of the identity until proven beyond reasonable doubt.

Illegitimate Identities   An illegitimate identity is when an attacker creates a principal for themselves or adds an additional backdoor credential to an existing principal. This technique provides the attacker a persistent identity that can be difficult to discover.

One way to find an illegitimate identity is by finding a characteristic or flaw whereby you can reliably discover their presence. For example, bouncers at night clubs check for fake IDs by checking hidden or difficult to reproduce aspects of a government ID card. Another way to identify illegitimate identities is through threat intelligence. For example, an attacker may use the same account name or other attribute when creating illegitimate identities within the system.

Another effective method for identifying illegitimate identities is through reconciliation with a trusted reference source. This method is best suited for technology systems where there is a central registration of all identities and a way to verify and revoke or invalidate illegitimate identities. A human resources database is one example of an effective source for linking active user principals with their user accounts.

Anomaly detection may also be able to identify abnormal user accounts in a highly consistent system. For example, differential analysis can be used to discover illegitimate identities if every component in the system has the exact same set of configured principals. That said, many systems suffer from one-off configurations or other anomalies which may make this method challenging. This is a great example of how complexity can be the enemy of security.

Proxied or Impersonated Identities   When an attacker uses proxied or impersonated identities it means that a component within the system has already authenticated and is performing (presumably illegitimate) activities on behalf of the attacker. This typically means one of three things:

- The attacker found and is exploiting a weakness within the system or one of its components.
- The attacker attained administrative authorization to a component which runs under a preestablished identity.

- The attacker previously exploited a vulnerability running under the compromised identity and compromised the integrity of the service by installing a backdoor which runs under the identity.

This may sound like it only applies to the technology world, but in reality this applies to human processes and physical security equally. For example, an attacker might socially engineer an employee to use their identity to perform an action on their behalf or extort a security guard to cause them to perform actions on their behalf (the extortion threat is essentially the backdoor in this case).

The important note about proxied or impersonated identities is that the attacker is not the one establishing the authentication; therefore, the underlying credential may not be compromised. That said, it is still very possible that the attacker may be able to use the compromised identity to obtain the credentials for the account if they are available.

Backdoor

A backdoor is a means of controlling the system or one of its components using a legitimate or illegitimate form of access. This is the aspect of the compromise which enables the attacker to perform arbitrary actions within the system, either using stolen credentials or under the identity of a vulnerable or compromised component.

The backdoor used by the attacker will typically be one of three types: abuse of a legitimate form of access, abuse of a component, or a purely malicious form of access. The type of backdoor determines what aspects can be used in hunting to find other potential accounts, backdoors, or communication channels.

For a capability to be considered a backdoor it must allow either remote control of the system, exfiltrate otherwise protected information beyond an edge, or allow the attacker to tamper with information from beyond an edge. Many tools and exploits used in an attack rely on the attacker having preexisting access to the compromised system or component and therefore are not considered backdoors. For example, lockpicks and lock shims might enable you to pick a lock on a door, but these rely on a preexisting form of access (the door). In contrast, a network tap that forwards captured traffic to an attacker's server hosted on the Internet compromises the edge of the service and allows the attacker to view otherwise protected information.

Abuse of a Legitimate Form of Access   In our first category, the attacker abuses an otherwise legitimate form of access to control the system or component. For example, the attacker might:

- Exploit a vulnerable human process to their benefit
- Log in through a VPN with stolen credentials
- Enter a building through an unlocked external door
- Access a victim's e-mail through a web portal or e-mail client
- Social engineer a user to perform an action on their behalf

In this case, there is nothing malicious about the means of access used by the attacker; therefore, nothing about the means of access can be used to identify other malicious activity. Instead, we must characterize the attacker's access and use attributes about the attacker's access to identify this activity elsewhere in the system. For example, we may be able to identify the attacker's communication based on their use of a specific phone number, IP address, user agent string, or other artifact. We may also be able to track the attacker by their authentication method by monitoring the user account, fake ID, or picture from a security camera.

Abuse of a Legitimate Component   The second category of backdoor occurs when the attacker abuses a legitimate capability to provide an illegitimate form of access. For this to occur, the attacker needs to first exploit a weakness in the system to gain initial access. Once exploited, the attacker can use a legitimate capability of the system or component against itself to provide a durable backdoor. For example, an attacker might:

- Add an email forwarding rule to the victim's mailbox to steal information
- Augment a legitimate business process to insert themselves in the middle
- Leave a cell phone in a secure facility allowing them to listen in on conversations

- Use a scripting engine to run malicious code using a command line parameter
- Abuse a legitimate application to execute arbitrary commands hosted outside of the system, a technique referred to living off the land, or LOL bins
- Use of an application vulnerable to DLL sideloading to load a malicious library to provide covert control, such as with DLL sideloading

When dealing with abuse of a legitimate component the actual malicious entity is the configuration in which it is used. For example, there is nothing wrong with the cell phone, scripting engine, or e-mail forwarding rule apart from its use to divert information or control to an untrusted entity outside of the system.

From a forensic\detection perspective, the first thing to consider is whether the legitimate capability is a common part of the system. You may be able to identify other backdoors if the capability is abnormal for the system or has a distinct attribute when used by the attacker.

If the capability is normal it will not be useful to search for the component itself because the majority of the times it will be benign. Instead, we must look for the combination of the component and its state. This could mean searching for persistence points, such as conditions which launch the component in this specific state automatically.

Malicious Form of Access   Our third category of backdoor is a purely malicious form of access implemented by the attacker. This is perhaps the most obvious and easy to understand of the three since there is no legitimate reason for the capability to exist.

A purely malicious form of access has no reasonable legitimate use and can be tracked based on any available identifying characteristic. Some examples of purely malicious backdoors include:

- Malware, such as Trojan backdoors, webshells, or other malicious remote control utilities
- Spies
- Phone or network taps or retroreflectors
- A tunnel into a secure facility

Communication

Communication is the path between the attacker and the backdoor. For an attacker to control a system they need some way to communicate with it. This communication path might be normal (a regular inbound connection, such as the exposed administrative capability), reverse (where the compromised component connects to the attacker), or proxied through an intermediary such as a command and control server.

Data

Data refer to the sensitive information which the attacker tampers with, steals, or destroys. This information will typically fit into at least one category of sensitive information from our "identify" chapter.

Data represent the real impact\loss to the organization and can be used to identify the motive of the attacker. The motive can be useful in identifying the attacker and determining other potential targets.

Persistence and Exposure

The ABCs of incident response provide a picture of identities and components which may have been interacted with by the attacker. That said, simply interacting with a system, component, or identity doesn't necessarily imply that it is compromised and needs to be rebuilt. For example, if an attacker pings every machine within a network once should that imply that every machine needs to be rebuilt? Likely not.

The key differentiator as to whether a system, component, or identity is compromised comes down to persistence. Most attackers will want to persist for two reasons.

First, persistence provides defense against incident response actions taken by the victim. Eviction will be unsuccessful while an attacker maintains some sort of covert control over the system. As such, establishing illegitimate forms of access, authorization, and\or authentication enables the attacker to protect themselves from losing all control over the victim's system.

Second, persistence can provide a "save point" within the victim's system. Many attacks require the attacker to spend a decent amount of time performing discovery and lateral traversal while the attacker gets their bearing within the environment. Once the attacker finds a key system or obtains a notably more powerful credential they may establish persistence as a shortcut back to that compromised system or identity.

Persistence provides the attacker the ability to circumvent normal access, authorization, and/or authentication by compromising system integrity or credential confidentiality. Once persistence is established, the only way to reestablish trust within the compromised system is to eliminate any known attacker persistence points, thereby restoring system integrity and credential confidentiality.

During incident response any relevant systems, components, and credentials should be categorized as either compromised or exposed based on evidence of persistence, interaction, or credential exposure.

Compromised

A system, component, or credential marked compromised implies that activities it performs should not be trusted for legitimate purposes due to evidence that it is no longer trustworthy. Anything listed as compromised must be addressed during the coordinated response effort to reestablish system integrity and/or credential confidentiality.

A system or component is deemed compromised if we have proof that the attacker has tampered with its integrity. In other words, we can assert that some form of persistence was established in the state of the system or component, whether that be through:

- Creation of a backdoor account
- Installation of an illegitimate form of access
- Modification to provide an illegitimate or compromised credential unintended authorization

From a credential perspective, compromise implies that the attacker has demonstrated their knowledge of a credential through evidence of its use. In other words, we can positively attribute malicious activity to a new authenticated session established using an illegitimately obtained credential. Examples include:

- Evidence that an attacker used a stolen or duplicated ID badge to pass through a secure door

- Creation of a new authenticated session within the system using a stolen credential
- Attempts to use a valid stolen credential against any system, regardless of its acceptance

Exposed

Exposed implies that the analyst has evidence that an attacker had both access and authorization to compromise a credential, system, or component, but there is no evidence of actual compromise. While there is no evidence of malicious use, the system, component, or credential should be considered for inclusion in the reclamation process if justified by potential impact.

One example of exposure occurs if an attacker interacts with a system or component without evidence that its integrity was tampered with. Examples of exposed systems or components might include an attacker:

- Accessing a file server to exfiltrate information but not installing a backdoor
- Interacting with employees of an organization but not showing evidence of an insider threat or coercion
- Logging on to a system or component using a legitimately published form of access but not creating an illegitimate backdoor

From a credential perspective, exposure implies that the attacker had the ability to compromise the confidentiality of a credential but that there is no proof that the attacker is aware of its availability. Exposed credentials imply that the attacker might know the credential and therefore it should be considered as part of a coordinated response, but the necessity of its change depends on the value of the credential and the risk tolerance of the organization. Examples of exposed credentials might include if an attacker:

- Was in a room containing a password list without evidence that it was read or photographed
- Accessed a system or component with a principal that could read credentials from other sessions without evidence that credential theft was performed

- Performed actions under an identity which had the ability to compromise its credential but without evidence that the credential was read

The purpose of the exposed categorization is to help the organization control the scope of a response while still tracking suspicious entities. As we will discuss in our next chapter, the scope of a response is based heavily on the risk tolerance for an organization.

Scoping the Compromise

Each time new malicious activity is detected, break it down into its components using the ABC model. Ask yourself questions such as:

- What identity was used to carry out the suspicious activity?
- Was there a different identity which led to the suspicious activity?
- Is it possible that the suspicious activity led to one or more compromised credentials?
- Are there any other suspicious activities which are similar or the same?
- Was there any persistence established as a result of the suspicious activity?
- What communication path led to the suspicious activity?
- Were there any abnormal communications performed because of the suspicious activity?
- Was any sensitive information involved in the suspicious activity?

Search for other activity which may be related to the newly discovered artifact each time a new element of the ABCs is found. Be sure to record every compromised or exposed system, component, and credential to help prepare for recovery.

One technique I found helpful is using a link analysis tool to delineate each element and how it is related to the incident at hand. Relationships between entities should contain the rationale as to why they are linked, and individual events should have the means of access, authorization, and authentication or exploitation used to achieve the objective.

Tracking

Implement detection each time you discover a new compromised account, backdoor, or communication channel. Tracking enables you to identify new suspicious activity and helps amplify prior investigation results.

Monitoring Attacker Assets

The highest fidelity form of tracking involves identifying attacker-unique assets. These assets include accounts, backdoors, and communication channels used solely for attack purposes with no legitimate use otherwise.

Interaction involving attacker-created accounts, backdoors, and communication channels provides a high-fidelity method of identifying previously unknown elements of the ABCs which will improve likelihood of a complete recovery.

Monitoring Compromised Accounts, Systems, and Components

Compromised assets have a perfectly legitimate use during normal system operation. In addition, they are likely to be rich sources of information about the attacker and their plans. Monitor anomalous activity involving any known compromised accounts, systems, and components to help unveil other previously undiscovered compromised assets and to help detect any new compromise.

Compromised assets are best monitored using anomaly detection or comparison to a historical baseline. Identify normal activities performed by these entities and investigate any significant deviations from their normal operation.

When performing this form of detection, remember that anomaly detection is the lowest fidelity technique and is likely to result in multiple false positive detections. Be sure to validate any suspicious behavior prior to deeming it malicious or identifying principals, systems, or components as being compromised.

Monitoring Tactics, Techniques, and Procedures

The third aspect of tracking involves detecting tactics, techniques, and procedures (TTP). These elements of the attack likely involve legitimate tools, capabilities, and activity abused for malicious purposes.

TTPs might include elements such as:

- Known interests of the attacker
- Legitimate services used by the attacker for communication or data exfiltration
- Legitimate tools or capabilities employed by the attacker
- Patterns of behavior which the attacker exhibits during their activity

These elements will vary in fidelity but can be valuable in monitoring attacker abuse of the system and uncovering additional ABCs.

The Art of Response

It is very easy to look at an incident and call anything touched by the attacker compromised; however, doing so means subjecting the organization to performing a bunch of unnecessary work. The real skill in response is seeing how narrow the scope can become.

Time is your enemy during an incident and when planning a coordinated response. Each moment spent in analysis paralysis or rebuilding machines unnecessarily is a moment that the attacker can compromise a new asset or get closer to impact or exfiltration. A skilled responder must effectively balance time spent on investigation and response with the risk of potentially missing something critical.

Response is a cyclical process which keeps looping until the growth of the list of compromised systems, components, and accounts begins to slow or stop. Notice I said compromised, not exposed. There is likely to be a constant stream of new exposed entities while the incident remains active.

Forensic Integrity

One important thing to keep in mind during response is the potential need for forensic integrity. Maintaining forensic integrity means ensuring:

- Any evidence of malicious activity is captured completely and in an unaltered state

- The integrity of any evidence can be proven
- The chain of custody for that evidence is maintained

During response, one of the challenges involves avoiding making unnecessary changes to entities involved in the incident. Each change performed runs the risk of damaging or destroying evidence which may be critical to investigation or prosecution.

Always determine whether legal prosecution is a possibility before performing any form of analysis on entities involved with an incident. If prosecution is possible, determine requirements for evidence collection prior to performing any analysis on compromised or exposed systems, components, or accounts.

Example: Catching Suspicious Activity on Camera

Imagine you identify an individual acting suspiciously in a secure facility using a security camera. Using the ABC model, we might start by trying to identify the individual based on the video. We also would want to know the way they got into the secure facility, so we would likely look at other security cameras to identify the path they took and any other previously undetected suspicious activity they performed along the way. These cameras would also provide a list of backdoors they used to ultimately gain access to the secured area where they were detected.

The suspect likely needed to perform some form of authentication to enter the various locked doors leading to the secured space, thus each of these would be considered an instance of authentication by the attacker. Tracking anywhere else these credentials were leveraged might identify other previously undetected activities. Additionally, these credentials should be compared to an authoritative list of valid identities to determine whether the identity being used is legitimate or a form of persistence.

Each time we capture the suspect on camera we should also be looking for evidence of data theft, tamper, or destruction (the data aspect). For example:

- Did the suspect steal or modify any documents?
- Did they photograph sensitive materials?
- Was anything important destroyed?

In addition, we should be looking for any attempts to establish persistence. For example:

- Do we see any suspicious changes made to security controls?
- Did the suspect install any form of remote monitoring capability?
- Do we have evidence of the suspect creating a new ID badge or other credential?

From a communication perspective, we may be able to identify a common path used by the suspect. Monitoring this path may be useful in determining if there are other individuals involved in this activity.

This process would collectively be referred to as a single security incident. Analysis would likely continue in this manner until ultimately you felt confident that there were no other significant elements missing. At that point, you would likely respond to the incident by catching the suspect, revoking any credentials they used, removing any illegitimate backdoors, and potentially blocking off the communication channel (if access was established using an illegitimate path).

Example: Cyberattack

Imagine you are a security administrator who suddenly receives an alert that suspicious activity is occurring on one of your servers or workstations. Upon investigation you validate that the activity is in fact malicious. The process launching the malicious activity seems to have a lot of delays and occasionally makes mistakes in the commands it runs, signaling that this might be a human operated attack.

Your first move will likely be to try and identify the parent process for all of this malicious activity – the backdoor. After some research you correlate most of the suspicious activity to an oddly named application which is configured to launch every time the system starts up. This application does not appear to be legitimate and, based on further research, is not common in the world. This is likely the attacker's backdoor.

Given its rarity, you determine that the backdoor is likely inherently malicious – in other words, the attacker is not abusing a legitimately-published capability or legitimate in-box component. This means that searching for the file should help you rapidly identify any other compromised systems in the enterprise. Sure enough, searching by the hash of the file reveals two more malware implants. All three of these systems can be fairly safely classified as compromised components.

Using the ABC model, you start looking for any accounts associated with the malware. The malware itself runs using a system account, but malware doesn't place itself there – something had to put it there. As you review authentication logs on the component you notice a strange user principal using a remote execution tool just moments before the malware appears. This user principal is the identity used for a public website run by the organization. Further research shows that it is also correlated with the other two malware implant installations and appears to have had a sudden spike in the number of systems it authenticated against in the recent past. We can fairly safely mark this account as compromised.

Now on to communications. We have a few paths to use here. First, the malicious backdoors you found don't operate autonomously – they need to receive commands from somewhere. An analysis of the network activity performed by the backdoors show an outbound connection to a strange website over SSL. You decide to search for other communications to this website and find a webserver, but this time the application is different – the application is a webserver accepting inbound network connections from the same address that is controlling the malware implants. We can now circle back to the backdoor aspect of the breach.

The malicious activities are being performed by the webserver's application and using the website's identity, which implies that the attacker may have found a way to run arbitrary commands using the website. A malware scan of the web published directory identifies a malicious web page flagged as a backdoor, and a search for the newly found backdoor identifies it in the same location on all of the webservers in a specific web farm. This implies one of two things: either the attacker has found a vulnerability within webservers in this farm or the attacker attained enough authorization to write this backdoor to the webservers and is using their direct exposure to the Internet as a simplified means of control. We can now mark all webservers in this web farm as compromised components.

Finally, a review of webserver logs identifies the initial date and time that the backdoor was written to the directory. In addition, we can identify communication made from the attacker's address around the time when the file was created to determine how the backdoor was installed. We can also analyze anomalous communications made by the webserver after the backdoor was installed to identify other potentially compromised endpoints or accounts.

11
RECOVER

Recovery can begin as soon as the first compromised account, back-door, communication channel, or compromised system or component is identified. The majority of effort during recovery is allocated to planning most of the time, thus it is good to get a head start on recovery efforts while response is still underway.

Your organization is almost definitely going to need recovery capabilities regardless of the amount of effort invested in secure system design. Human error, design oversights, third-party component vulnerabilities, first party code vulnerabilities, natural disasters, and a variety of other conditions might cause your once secure system to require recovery.

This chapter will have a noticeable slant towards recovery of technology systems given that many of the tools and techniques only practically exist in that space (could you imagine photocopying every piece of paper in an organization and shipping it to a giant vault monthly?). Where possible, we will reach back to the physical and human process worlds for comparison.

Documenting Recovery Processes

Your recovery team is going to want instructions on how to quickly reestablish core systems during an incident. Every critical system design should include instructions on how to recover its operation in the event of an incident. Be sure to include aspects such as:

- An estimate on the amount of time each major phase of recovery takes
- Skill or role dependencies, especially if external consultants or vendors are required to restore operation
- External dependencies which must be restored prior to the system

- System interdependencies, such as if one component within the system needs to be restored before another

Once developed, be sure to update and test the recovery plan periodically. One of the worst findings during an incident is when you attempt to use a recovery plan only to find that the steps don't work or are based on an antiquated version of the system.

Preparing for System and Component Recovery

Reestablishing capabilities provided by services tends to be one of the main focuses during recovery. The ability to get everything back online in a secure fashion will significantly depend on the organization's understanding of the system, its dependencies, and authentication infrastructure.

Dependencies

Perhaps the most important aspect of recovering a system is knowing any dependencies it has. A system's dependencies determine the order that restoration occurs and helps identify the critical path to service recovery.

Identifying dependencies helps discover any susceptibilities a system may have. For example, dependency analysis may uncover that a critical service or component relies on an outside capability that may not have previously been identified as critical. This may lead to a change in the priority of the dependent system or result in a redesign of the service to eliminate the dependency.

Dependencies are not always technical or operational. Sometimes a dependency may be on a specific skillset which may be outsourced to an outside organization such as a support contract or consultant. Another example might be a single individual who knows a credential. Knowing these dependencies enables you to address risk early before an incident occurs.

Document Build Steps

Another key part of ensuring effective service restoration is documenting any steps required to build a new instance of the service. Service or component rebuilds are commonplace during a recovery effort and will likely be necessary if a destructive attack takes place. These plans are also important should the integrity of the service or one of its components justify rebuild.

The level of detail used in build steps is likely to vary between systems. Including too much detail quickly makes the process antiquated and intolerant of minor changes which occur through natural system evolution. That said, high-level plans leave room for error and may cause inconsistency in the newly recovered service.

Preparing for Information Recovery

Information recovery is typically all about backups. Many times good backups are typically what truly save the day in the event of an outage – assuming they were implemented correctly. Backups can include an entire functioning system or only data for restoration into a new instance of a system depending on need. Proper backups can quickly reestablish availability, validate system or component integrity, and sometimes provide forensic artifacts for investigation which may have been tampered with or destroyed by the attacker.

There are multiple types of backups that an organization may choose to utilize, each with its own set of benefits and drawbacks. In this section we will cover these various techniques and some of their key differentiators.

Backup Metrics

There are two main metrics to keep in mind when designing a backup strategy: Recovery Time Objective (RTO) and Recovery Point Objective (RPO).

RTO refers to the amount of time your organization is willing to wait while systems are restored. This essentially governs how much information is backed up at a given time. For example, backing up the entire system during every interval provides the quickest RTO, but does so at the cost of an amazing amount of storage.

RPO determines the amount of data you are willing to lose if you had to resort to restoring from backup. The RPO dictates how often backups of the system are performed, with the acceptable loss being the period between backups.

Traditional Backups

A traditional backup strategy makes a copy of a system, component, or its information and stores it until it is needed. Traditional backups work in almost any situation and are a tried-and-true strategy for restoring the integrity and availability of lost, corrupted, or tampered information.

On the negative side, a traditional backup strategy typically wastes a lot of time and effort backing up unchanged information. Your system might store additional copies of the same unchanged information each time a backup is made, therefore incurring unnecessary storage cost.

The alternative to backing up every file is to perform partial backups of only what has changed since the last full backup was performed. This technique trades RTO for storage cost, but typically enables more frequent backups thereby reducing RPO.

Journaling

Journaling is a technique where the system logs all changes made to the data. A journal can be very helpful in a number of situations, such as restoring from data corruption, forensics, and recovery from destructive or integrity attacks. This technique is most commonly employed with databases and storage volumes.

When an attack occurs, the journal can be replayed to recreate each activity that occurred up until the attack. This technique is commonly paired with a traditional backup strategy to limit the amount of logs that need to be retained.

A journal can also be used in forensics to identify attacker activity. Since any changes made to the dataset are logged, any attack activity performed on the information will be logged as well (assuming their changes occurred through the normal communication path for transactions).

In computer science, journaling is a key component in ensuring a system maintains its ACID status. ACID stands for atomicity, consistency, isolation, and durability and reflects the four properties of a system which guarantees data validity despite errors, corruption, or other unplanned integrity impact.

The most major drawback in journaling pertains to resource impact. Proper journaling requires a record corresponding with any change in the dataset. This means that any changes should be committed to the journal prior to being committed to the data. In other words, the additional overhead of journaling will likely slow the system down and may require additional resources to maintain the same level of performance.

In addition, journaling can require a significant amount of storage since a record of all transactions must exist. Some systems, like most enterprise database platforms, will combine traditional backups with journaling to archive old copies of the journal thereby capitalizing on cheaper long-term storage and freeing up space.

Lag Copies

A lag copy is when multiple instances of the same information exist with changes to at least one copy intentionally lagging behind the current production dataset. If something happens to the production dataset, the lag copy can be used to restore the information to the production dataset or help identify what changes happened which led to the outage. This technique is good for rapid recovery from corruption or destructive attacks since the lag copy is typically online.

The major challenge of using a lag copy is that the impact needs to be identified before the lag copy is overwritten. If not, the lag copy may be overwritten with the destroyed or corrupted information, thereby preventing recovery.

Versioning

Versioning is somewhere in the middle of traditional backups and a lag copy. Versioning is a technique that records changes to data over time, marking each formally captured change as a version. If an issue is encountered, the current version can be traced back to identify any changes made to the information and enable restoration of a previous working version or update to the current version to fix the issue.

Versioning works on information that has a very clearly defined change period, such as documents, configurations, or source code. Applying versioning to data that is constantly changing, like a database, is essentially journaling and anything less than isolating every change is essentially a very frequent traditional backup.

Protecting Your Backups

Backups are one of those technologies which tend to be overlooked until a crisis occurs, likely because they don't contribute directly to functionality of the service. In a crisis, backups can quickly rise to the top of the priority list. As such, it is extremely important to ensure their isolation from any attack or other impact which might affect the systems they protect.

Service Design

Perhaps one of the biggest mistakes in designing a backup solution is sharing infrastructure with any production service it protects. From an access perspective, design an edge between the backup service and any services it protects. Isolating the backup service helps protect it from a breach of any other service.

Authorization and authentication used to access a backup system should be separate from the identity design used to manage the system or its components. This design ensures that compromise of the system does not directly lead to a compromise of the system which controls its backups. Where possible, consider deriving all administrative principals to the backup service from a domain that is local to the backup service itself. If this is not possible, avoid routine exposure of principals with administrative authorization to the backup service outside of the system.

Backup Location

Another important consideration in backup design is the physical location of backup data. In many cases, you may want to have backup information stored in more than one location – one near to the system and the other distant.

Having backup data near the system typically provides faster recovery due to the reduced distance information must travel for restoration. These backups are typically online to enable change comparison or provide rapid recovery of corrupted or destroyed information.

Backups are also typically stored in a geodistant location from the service it protects. This approach helps protect information from large scale disasters which affect a sizeable geographic region. Depending on the RTO requirements these backups may be either online or offline.

Planning for Authentication Recovery

Authentication recovery involves two main processes: identification of illegitimate principals and validating that only intended individuals, systems, and components know any associated credentials. This rather tedious process is best planned for ahead of time to enable rapid reconciliation during recovery.

Identifying Illegitimate Principals

One of the challenges of any authentication system is ensuring proper identity lifecycle management, or ILM. This process involves provisioning, maintaining, and deprovisioning any identity used within the authentication service. Without ILM, an organization is likely to be incapable of rapidly identifying illegitimate principals in the event of an incident. This can result in the attacker maintaining control over the system through an undiscovered identity.

Ensure principals within your system are accompanied by enough identifying information to enable validation in the event of an incident. This should include human and nonhuman principles used within the system without exception. Any exception to this process may result in indecision about the impact of eliminating a potentially important principal.

In addition, principals should contain sufficient information to enable them to be compared to a source of organizational truth. Many times, this source of truth will be an HR database, partner registration, customer list, or change request used for creation of the principal.

In case of an incident, compare all principals associated with a compromised domain to their associated source of truth. Any unverifiable principals should be treated as suspicious and investigated as potential attacker activity.

Planning for Credential Control

The second part of planning for authentication response involves validating and reestablishing credential confidentiality. Loss of credential confidentiality undermines the trust inherent to authorization security and the process used to restore credential confidentiality has a direct impact on the amount of trust you can place in that principal's authenticity going forward.

Invalidating the Current Credential   Part of reestablishing control over a compromised principal includes invalidating the current credential. The approach used for this will depend on whether the compromised credential uses symmetric or asymmetric principles.

Invalidating a symmetric credential requires changing or removal of the compromised credential from the principal in the authentication system. This is typically performed by resetting the credential or shared secret with a new one unknown to the attacker.

Asymmetric credentials require revocation to be implemented as part of their design to enable invalidation. This is because most asymmetric credentials rely on trust chained from a digital signature made by a more authoritative source, such as in a PKI. While you could technically invalidate all credentials signed by that authority, this approach is likely going to be more disruptive than useful and should only be taken if the authority's credential is compromised. Always ensure that any asymmetric credentials have a means of invalidation built into identity design to limit the impact of compromise.

Credential Reissuance   One of the greatest challenges involved with recovery is credential reissuance. This is because we are no longer able to trust the authenticity of any actions performed by a compromised credential, and thus cannot use the credential as a means of confidentially transmitting a new credential to the individual, service, or component which legitimately uses the principal.

Prepare a plan for credential reissuance in the event of a widespread compromise. The plan should involve identifying users based on credentials issued from a completely separate domain. Consider using credentials which are issued from a domain that grants no administrative authorization to users from an outside domain, and ideally one which uses a strict credential issuance procedure. For example, certificates issued to a smart card provide strong security, asymmetric authentication, and protect the private key from exposure.

Another option might include printing an emergency credential on employee ID badges which is not disclosed until needed, or using employee personal cell phone numbers to issue a one-time authentication credential out-of-band. The goal is to utilize a credential whose confidentiality cannot be compromised using any identity issued by a compromised system.

As a last resort, manual authentication can be used to validate identities. While effective, this process is extremely slow and does not scale well. If this must be used, consider delegating this capability to multiple personnel throughout your organization to improve efficiency.

Credential Multiplicity If credential multiplicity is supported by your authentication system you may be able to simply invalidate an individual credential without disabling the principal associated with it. Remember that there can be a layer of abstraction available between principals and credentials. This abstraction can enable you to limit the impact of a compromise by disabling only the compromised credential.

For example, in many Bring Your Own Device (BYOD) systems a different certificate is issued to each device a user has. This model enables invalidation of specific credentials without completely disabling the user. This is a much more flexible model that also enables you to identify the likely source of a compromise based on the device the credential was issued to.

Validating Trusts

Trusts are a potential source of identity persistence, especially when principles authenticated across the trust are granted a default level of authorization (such as by registering a certificate as a trusted root certificate authority). Because of this, an attacker may modify a domain's trusts enabling them to maintain authentication using principals belonging to a domain they control.

Trusts will not change often in most systems and are likely to be highly standardized. Maintain a list of trusts required for the system to operate to enable detection of malicious entries during recovery.

Planning for Authorization Recovery

Authorization is an often-overlooked aspect of recovery planning, in part due to the potential effort involved. There are various lengths that you can go to when verifying authorization recovery, and each system and organization is likely to have their own balance of effort and risk tolerance.

Know Where Authorization Can Be Granted

The first step of planning for authorization recovery is knowing all the places where it can be granted. The difficulty of this effort greatly depends on whether the system under analysis involves physical, human process, or technology components.

Physical systems tend to be rather simple when it comes to authorization control, typically employing only pass–fail authorization based on a credential. More advanced systems might employ only a few levels of authorization and thus are still relatively simple to analyze. These more advanced systems are likely to be aided by technology to facilitate authorization decisions, but still tend to have fewer delegations than other types of systems.

Authorization controls in human processes tend to be slightly more complex than those employed in physical systems. In human processes, delegations are typically made based on position within the organization or project and are aided by human discernment. Many times, authorization is granted by organizational delegation in human processes and is sometimes backed by documentation.

Technology systems tend to be the most complex when it comes to the number of authorization control locations, many times having thousands to millions of individual locations where authorization can be granted, and at a variety of levels (application, platform, operating system, and underlying infrastructure). This makes recovery challenging since a single obscure permission change may reduce the security posture of the system to almost nothing – another example of how complexity works against secure design.

For complex systems you will likely need to rely on the expertise of engineers involved with the design and management of the system or product support to know which configurations to pay attention to.

Compare Suspect Systems and Components to a Trusted Baseline

One way to help quickly identify suspicious delegations during recovery involves maintaining a trusted baseline for comparison. This is most effective for technology systems where automation can easily export these configurations for quick comparison. Ideally, the baseline should be updated with each major change made to the system to ensure accuracy during recovery efforts.

Going back to our secure design concepts, this comparison relies on the immutable aspect of system design. It is much easier to find anomalous configurations when a system and its components are highly consistent. Again, try to implement an edge between high value systems and their users or dependencies to help maintain consistency.

Verify Legitimate Authorization

We discussed the concept of time-limited authorization in our chapter on protection. One of the benefits of this practice is that it provides a list of all approved authorization requests along with their associated rationale. During recovery, review the list of authorization granted to the system to identify any suspicious rationale or authorization grants which do not correspond with the approved list.

Test Incident Response and Recovery Plans

One of the biggest mistakes an organization can make is not testing their recovery plans. Usually, this mistake is highlighted when the organization encounters a major breach and finds themselves unable to restore critical data or reestablish trust in their system.

Ideally, recovery testing should include every key player in the organization from the executive level down to rebuilding or restoring the system from backups. This process helps proactively identify any gaps in planning and ensures that backups are functioning properly and that the data being captured is valid and usable. In addition, this enables leadership to realize exactly how long a typical recovery effort takes in the event of a real breach.

Seek Outside Perspective

Consider bringing in an outside consultant to help perform incident response and recovery testing. Consultants provide an outside perspective and are usually aware of the most recent attack trends and techniques. This can provide a great training opportunity for your staff while providing an opportunity to see how your organization would perform when faced with real attack scenarios.

The Recovery Process

Responding to an incident is an active process with new compromised accounts, systems, and components appearing throughout. The recovery process should begin once the first compromised system, component, or credential is identified and be constantly added to as new information is fed in by the response process. Starting recovery in parallel is ideal for reducing the amount of time that the system is in a compromised state and provides the attacker the least amount of time to respond to recovery efforts.

The recovery process should be relatively quick where possible, measured in days or weeks and not months. The longer an attacker remains within the system the more likely they are to identify detection, response, and recovery efforts.

Focus on efforts that directly impact the attacker. The ABCs of incident response identifies the key elements of the incident which provide the attacker control; thus, all recovery efforts should have a direct tie back to intercepting a compromised account, a backdoor, a communication channel, or reestablishing control over data.

While it may be tempting to fix security issues you come across during the recovery process, this practice only serves to delay reclamation.

Instead, add any identified security improvements to a backlog for future efforts post-recovery.

Normal Recovery Process

Try to avoid unnecessary interruptions to service where possible if there is no sign of imminent danger posed by the attacker's presence within the system. This may not always be possible given that the recovery process is by nature disruptive, but drastic actions may cause more harm than good if there is no evidence of impending catastrophe. That said, always have an emergency recovery plan ready should conditions change.

A normal recovery process begins by first determining the steps involved in recovering any services compromised by the attacker and determining the order which they should be recovered based on dependencies. Many times, these services can be rebuilt or recovered in parallel to the production service thereby reducing downtime.

Eviction occurs after planning and preparation is complete. If performed properly, the attacker will suddenly find all of their credentials, backdoors, and communication channels unusable – effectively pushing them all the way back out of the system. Eviction should be the last step in a normal recovery process.

Emergency Recovery Process

Sometimes the risk posed by attacker presence outweighs the operational benefit of the system. For example, losses due to system downtime may be acceptable if there is evidence that the attacker is preparing for a highly destructive form of impact. In these scenarios the recovery process essentially happens backwards starting with eviction.

In an emergency recovery, compromised credentials, systems, and components are taken offline to preserve system integrity while recovery occurs. This approach typically results in reduced system functionality or significant downtime.

If an emergency recovery process is initiated, ensure that all systems remain offline until recovery is completed. This action will almost certainly notify the attacker that you are aware of their means of control. Bringing systems online prematurely is likely to cause the attacker to use any residual control to immediately change tactics (their ABCs) and maintain presence.

Interception

The goal of interception is to reestablish credential confidentiality and system integrity by eliminating the attacker's ABC's of incident response. Interception should always be the first thing you plan during a recovery since it enables the emergency recovery process if it becomes necessary.

The most important aspect of interception is the order that the ABCs are eliminated. The attacker can circumvent normal access, authorization, and authentication processes if they maintain control over illegitimate backdoors within the system. This can cause them to obtain new credentials if they notice that their current credentials are suddenly invalidated.

Just the same, starting interception by removing backdoors may cause the attacker to use what credentials they have against any legitimate means of access they have available. This will "tip your hand" to the attacker and informs them which backdoor techniques you are aware of. In addition, the attacker will maintain control if backdoor elimination is not comprehensive. In either of these cases the attacker is likely to respond by changing their backdoor technique (and likely their communication channel) to maintain control over the system.

Always start interception by eliminating attacker communication channels. By cutting their ability to communicate with backdoors the attacker can no longer circumvent normal access and authorization, and they are forced to use only publicly available means of access. If done properly, effectively pulls the rug out from under them leaving them scrambling to reestablish control through publicly available means of access.

Intercepting Communications

When intercepting attacker communication channels, ensure that your approach is comprehensive. Interception should be performed at all service edges as well as locally for each component. This is especially important with technology systems where laptops and other mobile devices are likely to enter and leave the enterprise network. An attacker can update or replace their backdoor if a compromised system leaves the network and connects to the attacker's communication channel via an outside network.

Interception should include as many means of blocking attacker communications as possible. These protections should be implemented at all edges and will vary depending on the technology available.

In the physical or human process world the solution basically means blocking suspicious or malicious individuals from accessing your system. This could include strategies such as:

- Blocking their ID badge from being able to access the facility
- Instructing security guards to be on the lookout for the malicious individual
- Posting a guard at the location where malicious communication occurs

Technology systems tend to be more complex since there are several ways for traffic to flow. Consider strategies such as the following:

- Blocking attacker IP addresses on firewalls
- Blocking attacker DNS names on proxy servers
- Creating an authoritative zone for attacker's DNS zones on internal DNS to block name resolution or redirect it for monitoring
- Using routing entries to block or redirect attempts to connect to an attacker communication channel
- Block the ability to route to attacker communication channels at each host using a firewall, routing entry, and/or hosts entry

Where possible, implement monitoring for connection attempts made using any known attacker communication channel. If there is no legitimate reason for use of the communication channel than any attempt to connect is either suspicious or malicious and should warrant immediate response.

Intercepting Authentication

To intercept authentication, we must reestablish credential confidentiality and invalidate any active authenticated sessions used by the attacker. If done properly, this change will reestablish trust in actions performed by principals and reduces attacker authorization to effectively nothing.

First, determine the scope of authentication interception. Every known compromised credential should be considered in-scope for recovery. You may also want to include any exposed credentials as part of the recovery effort in the event that the attacker obtained them and just hasn't used them.

Some organizations may choose to change all administrative credentials as a part of this process regardless of evidence of compromise. This practice may be disruptive to operations but increases the likelihood of a successful recovery.

Depending on the organization's risk tolerance, you might also consider all other credentials within the system as part of this process. The return on investment of resetting nonadministrative credentials will vary depending on the impact to operations and many times may not be warranted.

Second, prepare the order and process for intercepting each targeted credential. Quantify the value of each compromised credential using the equation from our chapter on authentication and plan to recover each credential in descending value order. The authentication recovery plan should include invalidation of any known compromised credentials as well as invalidation of any potentially attacker-controlled sessions made with the associated principal.

Third, develop a process for credential reissuance. This process should involve authenticating the appropriate user of the principal and securely setting or issuing the individual or service its new credentials. This process used for credential issuance should not trust any potentially compromised credential as a form of authentication for credential reissuance, but rather perform new authentication using a trustworthy out-of-band process.

Be sure to consider the scale of operations when designing a credential reissuance strategy. Large-scale credential reissuance can be a logistical nightmare and execution will likely require a significant amount of coordination and resources. In addition, remember that during response and recovery you may not be able to use normal communication channels.

Intercepting Backdoors

Many times, successful interception of attacker communication channel will prevent an attacker from using backdoors to tamper with the system. Systems and components should be taken offline regardless of whether you believe that communication interception was successful in case you may have missed something during investigation or communication interception was not comprehensive.

While backdoors are third in order of risk during a recovery, many times interception can be performed in parallel to authentication interception. Once taken offline, these systems and components should not be restored to service until the entire recovery effort is complete. This is especially important if the organization chooses the emergency recovery process since the organization is likely to feel the immediate pain of service outage and may be inclined to restore system operation. Restoring a known compromised system or component to operation prior to fully executing the recovery plan may place the system at significant risk of compromise paired with a change in attacker persistence mechanisms, thus returning their stealth.

Operational Recovery

Operational recovery restores trust in a system to the best extent possible or acceptable after an incident. This process includes identifying dependencies as well as rebuilding or restoring components and information to enable production use of the service.

Operational recovery planning can occur in parallel to interception planning but should not be prioritized above interception. This is designed to ensure that there is always a plan to intercept and cut off attacker control at a moment's notice should there be evidence that a highly destructive attack is being planned or executed. That said, operational recovery has a much higher value proposition than interception in that it enables the service to be restored to operation confidently.

Assessing Impact

Our first step in operational recovery is determining the scope of recovery based on the list of compromised credentials, systems, and components from response. Each compromised asset should have an associated impact assessment which identifies the realized and potential impact to system and data security based on the attacker's available access and authorization.

Knowing the impact of the incident enables you to determine the recovery steps required to reestablish trustworthy operation. Be sure to highlight any unnecessary access, credential exposure, excessive authorization grants, and system or component logic vulnerabilities which led to the compromise as well as any confidentiality, integrity, or availability sensitive information which was impacted as a result.

Critical Hardening

The critical hardening phase is when you identify and stage any important configuration changes which render the system indefensible against the attacker. These should not be compliance or best-practice focused changes, but rather direct paths from an exposed component to administrative authorization that would render the recovery effort ineffective. For example:

- Preventing administrative credentials from exposure to at-risk components
- Reducing administrative authorization of a credential that must be exposed to at-risk components
- Addressing a vulnerability that enables an attacker to bypass authentication and remotely obtain administrative authorization without requiring an administrative credential
- Eliminating or reducing access to risky services traversing an edge

Where possible, these changes should be staged and implemented as part of interception to avoid notifying the attacker that you are aware of their presence. In information systems, an ideal way to accomplish this is through scripting or other forms of automation. The less time that an attacker has to detect and respond to your recovery the less likely they will be able to craft a timely retort.

Restoring Identity

Security in identity relies on domain integrity and credential confidentiality. Domain integrity means that we can trust that the domain's authentication decisions are accurate and that the principals it authenticates are authentic (i.e., there are no illegitimate principals created by an attacker). Credential confidentiality means ensuring only intended entities can authenticate as a security principal. If any systems or components involved with authentication or an administrative credential to the domain is deemed compromised, the domain should be considered compromised as a result.

Once compromised, we lose trust in any principals the domain authenticates and the security of any securables it protects. As such, we cannot confidently recover any service leveraging authorization controls without first recovering any domain which supplies it authentication or authorization services.

Scoping Identity Recovery   To begin, list out any known compromised domains. A domain should be considered compromised if any of the following conditions are true:

- Integrity of the domain is considered compromised
- A component with the ability to affect credential confidentiality or domain integrity is considered compromised
- An account with administrative authorization to the domain is considered a compromised account
- In high security systems, if any credential associated with a principal having administrative authorization to the domain is considered an exposed account

Once compromised, any symmetric credentials used for authentication by the domain should be considered at high risk of being exposed. This happens because symmetric authentication requires the credential or a symmetric equivalent to be stored for comparison. Depending on how your organization chooses to handle exposed accounts this may affect your recovery plans for other domains.

Next, build a matrix that lists any domains that trust a compromised domain for authentication or authorization. This matrix will help determine the order that recovery will need to take place as well as the potential impact of the compromised domain and any information or systems that may have been put at-risk as a result.

Recovery should always begin with the most trusted domain and cascade downwards through the trusts to the least trusted ones. If multiple trust chains exist, these recovery efforts can be performed in parallel if resources allow.

Recovering a Compromised Domain   To recover a compromised domain, we must reestablish trust in:

- Integrity of the system and its underlying components
- Authenticity of principals authenticated by the domain
- Confidentiality of any credentials associated with principals having administrative authorization to the domain, the system, or any of its components

Begin your authentication recovery plan by listing out all compromised domains, compromised credentials, and any compromised component that is part of a service that provides authentication or authorization. This list will be the basis for the scope of domain recovery efforts.

Decommission any compromised components involved with authentication or authorization when recovery begins. This change helps ensure that any compromised component with an undetected communication channel or secondary backdoor cannot be used to reestablish control over the domain during or after recovery.

Next, change any credentials which provide administrative authorization to the domain. Some organizations might consider changing credentials for principals not deemed exposed or compromised unnecessary, but keep in mind that a compromised domain could enable the attacker to discreetly obtain a credential or equivalent which may be able to be used to reestablish control over the domain.

Remember that credential multiplicity may enable a single principal to have multiple credentials. This may enable an attacker to persist by adding an additional credential to a legitimate principal. To be safest, ensure invalidation of all credentials associated with administrative principals.

Third, invalidate any existing sessions with administrative authorization to the domain regardless of compromised or exposed status.

This change helps ensure any previously established attacker sessions are no longer of value. When paired with the previous credential change this should remove any administrative control the attacker has over the domain.

Finally, reset the credentials for any remaining compromised accounts and invalidate any active sessions. Some organizations may also choose to perform these actions on exposed accounts to ensure comprehensive recovery.

Recovering Compromised Systems and Components

Our next phase of recovery focuses on the nonidentity aspects of the system. This phase of recovery begins by reestablishing trust in the integrity of its components. A system's integrity relies on the integrity of its components, and therefore the success of the recovery effort is predicated on reestablishing trust in the integrity of its components. Plan to recover or decommission any components of the system deemed compromised during response.

While recovery of components can begin in parallel with identity where resources allow, the newly recovered service should not be made available for use until its identity components are fully recovered.

If multiple systems need to be recovered, there are two aspects which decide the order in which recovery occurs. The first is organizational impact – a higher impact service should be restored prior to a lower impact service to minimize operational impact. Remember that the impact of service availability and integrity is an organizational measure and that it may not always follow the complexity involved in restoring the service.

The second aspect to consider is dependency. Many services will be interdependent and may require one service to be fully restored before another can even begin. Approach dependency mapping in the same way that we mapped trusts in domains – create a matrix which identifies any intersystem dependencies and identify the critical path towards restoration of the most impactful services.

Recovering Components   From a component perspective, recovery is all about reestablishing trust in integrity. This integrity is derived from our ability to trust the decisions and actions made by the component, which in turn means we need to eliminate any illegitimate control over the component – the attacker-created backdoors that caused it to be flagged as compromised in the first place.

While an attacker backdoor can simply be removed, compromised components should always be rebuilt from scratch. In complex components, such as any in the technology realm, there are an unbelievable amount of minute changes which may provide an attacker a covert backdoor which may have gone undetected during response. Therefore, it is always better to rebuild the component from scratch whenever possible.

In our protect chapter we discussed the value of following the D.I.E. triad in system design, where a system and its components should be designed to be distributed, immutable, and ephemeral. Recovery of components designed following the D.I.E. model is typically simple – destroy the instance and create a new one if necessary. In contrast, traditional recovery may require days of investment as each component and its dependency is painstakingly rebuilt from scratch.

Avoid making any changes to the production components that may materially affect the attacker's control if interception has not yet been performed. Significant changes may notify the attacker that you are aware of the compromised system and cause them to change their persistence locations or types to remain resident. If this occurs, you may be pushed back from recovery to detection as new backdoors, compromised credentials, and compromised components begin to surface.

Another important consideration when rebuilding compromised components is avoiding migration of any attacker persistence in the process. Remember that you are rebuilding the component because you cannot trust its integrity, and therefore any content on that component should be considered suspect. Where possible, consider building a new instance of the component or restoring it from a trusted backup prior to the attack. If this is not possible, be sure to analyze any content moved from the system for any indicators of compromise – especially if the content can be used to provide control, such as active web content.

Recovering Systems   Begin restoring the system once the individual components of a system and its identify infrastructure are restored. System restoration involves recovering the operational interconnection between each component – essentially, the fabric that weaves the individual pieces into a system enabling it to function as a unit.

Unlike components, systems may be too complex to build from scratch. If so, we must be confident that detection and response processes identified any backdoors within the system. Consider comparing the system to previous backups to identify any inconsistencies as part of recovery to help improve this confidence.

Restoring Data   Our last step when recovering a compromised system is restoring its data. This process for restoring data is going to be heavily dependent on how the system works, thus difficult to cover at a high level.

The most important thing to consider during this process is once again ensuring you do not accidentally restore any attacker backdoors and artifacts as part of the process. Always analyze data being restored against any known attacker indicators of compromise – especially if the data can provide any form of control.

12
CLOSING

We exist in an ever more connected society with many of the most important aspects of our life tied to systems which we are forced to trust. This world does not wait for perfection before implementation; thus, it is critical that we understand the "why" behind each design decision we make.

I hope this book has provided you a new perspective, one that helps unify your understanding of security and helps you to better tackle the many challenges of defending a system in today's world. It is the work product of security professionals of today who define our trust in the world tomorrow, and we're going there no matter whether we trust everything or not.

Index